Movers & Shakers

Movers & Shakers

Women Making Waves in Spirits, Beer, and Wine

Hope Ewing

The Unnamed Press
Los Angeles, CA

The Unnamed Press
P.O. Box 411272
Los Angeles, CA 90041
Published in North America by The Unnamed Press.
FIRST EDITION
1 3 5 7 9 10 8 6 4 2

ISBN: 9781944700645

Copyright © 2018 by Hope Ewing

Cataloging in Publication is available upon request.

Distributed by Publishers Group West

Designed & typeset by Jaya Nicely
Cover Photograph by Oriana Koren

Table of Contents

For Tuan Lee, on the rocks, with a grapefruit twist
1½ ounces Diplomatico
½ ounce Batavia Arrack
¾ ounce Byrrh
¼ ounce Bigallet China-China

Theresa felt strange being there. However much she might have read in recent years about women in bars, they were still in her mind very much a male preserve, an almost magical kind of place where men went to get away from women.

—Judith Rossner, *Looking for Mr. Goodbar* (1975)

Feminism ain't about equality
It's about reprieve.

—Ani DiFranco, "Reprieve" (2006)

Foreword

I've met some of the most interesting and important women in my life in bars—behind them, sitting at them, or just standing around outside of them. There is something about a communal space, in that post-dusk allure of a night open with possibilities, that attracts fascinating people. I've met women who are athletes, writers, artists, parents, academics—sometimes all at the same time. I've overheard the musical preferences of cultural icons and women comparing salaries, wondering how to ask for the pay they deserve. I've seen women in recovery gracefully navigate their way through a night out with friends, and I've marveled at the accomplished way millions of women get out of bad dates.

Working in the spaces where people gather has brought so much meaning to my life. Being part of the magic that makes someone—anyone—feel welcome, however difficult their day or however dark the time, is a privilege I take very seriously. I love that my work requires a sustained, collaborative openness. I love having that kind of engagement with others in my community, with visitors from the other side of the world, and with my colleagues. I love how each day is so emotionally similar, but no two days are exactly the same.

My hospitality journey has been about nothing if not about meeting fascinating women. What I love most about Hope Ewing's book is that it's an introduction to so many of them. In *Movers and Shakers*, Hope has interviewed some of the most brilliant, creative, and innovative women in the business. These conversations are so alive, and they crackle with all the enthusiasm and joy these experts bring to the field. So much ground is covered in these pages, from desexualizing the workplace, to the agricultural art and science of making wine, to how these women make successful livings selling the products they make.

It's affirming and reassuring to see so many fascinating figures in the industry tell their stories and share their observations so candidly. The best part about meeting a fascinating woman is being delighted by what you learn from her, and reading this book provides the same kind of thrilling discovery. In *Movers and Shakers*, you'll learn the true meaning of hustle, the importance of mentorship; you'll see how productivity can bloom out of necessity or grief. There are lessons here about how to ask for money and how to reinvent a career. Mainly, though, *Movers and Shakers* shines a light on tenacity, professionalism, and entrepreneurship, all the complex and artful qualities women need to succeed not just in the beer, wine, and spirits industries, but everywhere.

Most important, though, these women are leading the way, machete-ing through the patriarchal jungle so that others can follow. As I read Hope's book, I kept returning to that essential saying about the first step in any successful journey: *You need to see it to be it.* Thanks to Hope Ewing and *Movers and Shakers*, more of us out there will see it.

— **Natalka Burian, July 2018**

Movers & Shakers

Introduction

"**W**hat's it like to be a woman in the industry?**"** is a terrible question. Imagine you are a rising star in the field you love, building a business, making a name. Now imagine, over and over again, people asking you not about your accomplishments but about your gender. As if it weren't enough to succeed against the added impediments of sexism and/or racism, you are tasked with qualifying your success.

This might come off a little militant for a book about booze. When I started writing it, it was early 2017. The country was reeling from the election, but few people knew what #MeToo meant. In the ensuing months, my little project to talk to women I admired in the beer, wine, spirits, and bar industries was suddenly in the midst of a major feminist moment. I came up with two objectives:

1. Dismantle "What is it like...?" This question is backward. It puts the onus on women to qualify their presence in male-dominated fields, when we should really be asking the industry leaders to explain other women's absence. The more women's stories we hear, the less anomalous it seems to have women tending bars, building brands, and running things. Which leads to the next objective.

2. Make a compendium of role models. Most if not all of those interviewed in the following pages had a person or people in their careers who showed them what was possible.

For many, these were people like Dale DeGroff, who mentored Julie Reiner, Audrey Saunders, and others in the craft of the cocktail, making the next generation of cocktail kings and queens. Others were women made famous by their work, like editor Talia Baiocchi, who set up a new kind of drinks magazine at the age of twenty-eight with an apparent immunity to internet hate, or writer Alice Feiring, who saw a problem and blew the lid off it. It is a consensus: representation is important. Once we know something is possible, it becomes imperative.

I did not want to ask the women in this book how they got here *despite* being who they are. I assumed that who they are—all the physical, emotional, and social factors that make up a woman's identity—was a key part of their success. What I really wanted to ask was: Who are these people with these fantastic jobs? How did they get to be so cool?

I have always been a late bloomer. Chalk it up to birth order, genetic predisposition, or old-fashioned indecision. I lost my last baby tooth at fifteen, and I've never been able to decide what I wanted to be when I grow up. After trying to make it work as a grant writer during my twenties, I left a budding nonprofit career to study creative writing. I thought an MFA would lead to a life in academia, and since I was terrible at office work, what did I have to lose?

Of course, now I know that even when you're starting from the bottom, you can still get a shovel and dig. When it became clear that the professor track was not going to pan out for me, I was already $80,000 deep in student loans, soon to have a master's degree in fiction, and no imminent career prospects. My stress nightmares at that time featured an oversize Suze Orman screaming, *"What were you THINKING?"*

Fortunately, that was also when I began bartending. Starting out as a server when I went back to school, I discovered I loved having a job where

I could move around, talk to people, and host the party every night. It scratched an itch I didn't know I had. By the time I was promoted to making drinks, I was hooked on the industry.

Working at a woman-owned Brooklyn neighborhood joint taught me how to pour and host—how to rule a room and bring people together. After graduating, I moved to Los Angeles, where I learned how to jigger and shake and chop a block of ice into glass-size rocks. I went deep. I devoured cocktail history and wine maps. I tasted everything put in front of me. My mind was blown, and I fit right in. The alcohol industries were going through renaissances, all within a decade or two of one another. Beer, cocktails, spirits, wine—they all had revolutions under way. Much of the time, women were at the forefront of change.

From ancient Sumer to today's mammoth Scotch distilleries, women have been a driving force in the production of intoxicating drinks. Women were brewers in ancient Egypt and Peru, and they distilled spirits in the Middle East and Europe since the invention of the alembic still by Maria Hebrea in ancient Alexandria.

Despite these and many other wholesome alcoholic pursuits, the predominant legacy in Western culture of women's dealings with alcohol stems from the eighteenth and nineteenth centuries. London's gin craze— eighteenth-century England's equivalent to the 1980s crack epidemic— established the concept of "mother's ruin." The dominant currencies of saloons in the American frontier in the nineteenth and early twentieth centuries were sex work and whiskey, and the two have since been linked in the popular consciousness. It was one of the ideas Prohibition was built upon: liquor was the corrupting poison used by women of the night to destroy (otherwise respectable) family men. When liquor was outlawed in 1920, imagine everyone's surprise when infidelity and spousal abuse stuck around.

After the repeal of Prohibition in 1933, laws concerning the production and sale of intoxicating spirits were left to each state to figure out, creating the foundation of "blue laws." These often prohibited women from tending bar, sitting at bars, or even entering a tavern through the front door in some places. Taverns were the preserves of men, where much of the important (and most fun) business of public life was conducted. It was as recently as 1971 that the California Supreme Court ruled that it was illegal to prohibit women from bartending.

Let that sink in for a moment. It was technically illegal to employ women as bartenders in California until 1971. Those of us born in the 1970s are just glimpsing middle age. The Old West conflagration of prostitution and booze is far from ancient history, and it's a legacy we are still trying to dismantle. As the beer, wine, spirits, and hospitality fields grow and change, women are stepping up to lead. Not content with the stereotype of the "chick bartender," hired for her looks to appeal to male clientele, they are opening their own bars and restaurants, starting consultancies, founding spirits brands, and more. As recently as 2007, women craft brewers were so underrepresented that brewmaster Teri Fahrendorf drove across the country collecting names, reassuring each woman she met that she was not, as previously assumed, the only one. She built a professional organization from this list of names dedicated to scholarship and mentorship, much like author and entrepreneur Deborah Brenner did when she took a hard look at the gender imbalance in winemaking in the mid-2000s and subsequently founded Women of the Vine & Spirits. Women have led by example and by helping each other.

This book is not meant to be comprehensive. For every woman I profile in these pages, there are a dozen more doing great work in the same field. I've tried, along the way, to refer to references for more in-depth information. My goal here is not to make a definitive list but to share their stories. Each person profiled here is doing their part to take down gender discrimination in the drinks business, intentionally or not, by doing what they love. From all-women bartending competitions to professional organizations to a global symposium on how to expand diversity initiatives, people are standing up and organizing. The future is female. More than a protest slogan, I've come to think of this phrase as an instruction. If we are to have a future, we have to step up.

Part One:
Making It

Romancing the Dirt

Like so many of my countrymen, I did not come to wine readily. In my early bar career in New York City's neighborhood pubs, the scene was all beer and whiskey. Unbeknownst to me, a revolution was going on, much of it centered right there in New York. It was a battle for the "soul" of wine, and it was fierce. Wines from Hungary, Slovenia, and Georgia were popping up on restaurant wine lists, and "orange" became an accepted descriptor. Biodynamic farming was transitioning from a hippie-dippie fringe element to a code for thoughtful, sustainable wine. All this, and I, like most other Americans, would be hard-pressed to tell you the difference between a Burgundy and a Bordeaux. And I'd *been* to Bordeaux.

The thing about wine that surely causes a lot of this kerfuffle is that there are so many pockets of knowledge and drastically different opinions, even among experts. For the casual drinker it can be overwhelming. There are the two- to five-dollar bottles that are treated with additives to make inexpensive wine palatable and consistent, and there are collectors' bottles that sell for thousands of dollars that one can only imagine contain the elixir of life. In between is a realm of mystery and shame, for most of us. It can be comforting to cleave to brand or grape loyalty, or simply revel in one's ignorance using smug populist rhetoric as a mask. These strategies make things simple, but they also close the door on something wonderful: delicious, delicious wine.

I could not remain ignorant after I moved to California in the 2010s. In America's grapevine heartland, everyone seemed to care about wine to some degree. I was scolded by a coworker for my clumsiness with a corkscrew at a neighborhood Lebanese restaurant, where I had my first LA serving job. Descriptions like "smooth," "harsh," and "husky" (huh?) were no longer sufficient. I actually needed to know what I was pouring. Luckily, Los Angeles in the 2010s was a superb place to learn, even as a broke server.

My then boyfriend and I started biking to independent wine shops a few times a week for tastings. We brought little notebooks and scribbled notes, taking cues from Madeline Puckette's beginner-friendly *Wine Folly* blog. Our studiousness made us staff favorites in no time. By the end of each event, we'd be wobbling back down the hills of Silver Lake with a few extra pours in our bellies and new ideas in our heads. Grapes with names like gamay and albariño existed, and they made wines that were "acidic," "grippy," "jammy," or "bright." There is a vocal contingent that loves to hate on wordy tasting notes, but I am a word person. Reading that a white carried hints of "stripper perfume" on the nose delighted me, especially when the light oak and white flowers brought on an intimate connection with the Vanilla Fields body spray I favored in middle school. The connection was a revelation, even when the wine was just okay. I wanted more, better ways to express this newfound fascination. Fortunately, Dr. Ann Noble took care of this in the 1970s.

If you've ever gone to a wine-tasting class and been handed a pie-shaped diagram, you're using a woman's contribution to the field. The first woman faculty member in the renowned University of California at Davis viticulture and enology program, sensory scientist Dr. Noble created the food-based lexicon of wine tasting and attendant Wine Aroma Wheel recognizable by novice tasters everywhere. In Bianca Bosker's book *Cork Dork*, the author describes a visit to Noble's home in Northern California and a session that involved adding canned asparagus, green peppers, dried apricots, and other common items to glasses of wine, imprinting each aroma in her sensory memory bank.

Noble pioneered the use of concrete, objective language to describe wine in lieu of the reigning language of the time, which included terms like "harmonious," "noble," "masculine," and "feminine." The exercise Noble put Bosker through was an abbreviated version of the course she developed in the 1970s, when UC Davis brought her in to improve its sensory evaluation curriculum. Noble's work redefined how we taste and think about wine for the next forty years.

In an interview with the *Gastropod* podcast, Bosker explained, "When we look at the history of the tasting notes they use to describe wine, they tend to reflect whatever values we happen to prize at that particular time." In a top-down, male-dominated social order, these values could be reliably skewed. Having relatively objective language—let's say, "grapefruit" or "lilies" instead of "feminine"—would appear to reflect a more egalitarian approach to appreciation. I, a plebeian, may not know what nobility tastes like, but I have had black tea and have smelled leather, and can recognize them in a glass. Having access to reasonably priced wine and a vocabulary with which to talk about it is crucial to the wine world. It is a boundless topic, one that with enough curiosity and education, anyone can come to enjoy.

Around the time Dr. Noble was changing the world at UC Davis, Napa Valley was emerging from its reputation as a bunch of unrefined cowboy winemakers to become a permanent force in global wine production. The infamous Judgment of Paris took place in 1976 and established Napa as an international contender. California's star was rising, but the women who flocked there to make wine were still facing 1970s sex discrimination. In Deborah Brenner's 2006 book, *Women of the Vine: Inside the World of Women Who Make, Taste, and Enjoy Wine,* she profiles twenty women working in California at that time. The book is a collection of Napa royalty, including Gina Gallo, Heidi Peterson Barrett (creator of, among other things, Screaming Eagle Cabernet), and Merry Edwards of the eponymous wine company. Their stories involve approaching family elders with the determination to take over the family business and facing discrimination from vineyard managers who scoffed at the very idea that a woman could do the physical work of the farm and the cellar. Amelia Morán Ceja of Ceja Vineyards relates her and her husband's struggle to establish their own vineyard and winery while raising young children, starting with an empty field and years of experience harvesting grapes alongside their families between school terms.

When I spoke to Deborah on the phone from her home in New York State, she was delighted to have been nominated that day for *Wine Enthusiast* magazine's 2017 Person of the Year award. She had been in the wine business for more than ten years but had really seen her advocacy work blossom over the past few. Deborah was inspired to write *Women of the Vine*, after a trip to Napa Valley while she was going through a divorce and considering a career change from her work in tech and PR, two heavily male-dominated fields. She met women whose hard-won careers in wine inspired her to promote their visibility within the industry. Role models, she told me, are vital. It's a refrain I heard from almost everyone: the more visible women are in a field, the more women will apply.

After the book, Deborah collaborated on Women of the Vine Wines, vintages made from a collective of women vintners in California. This lasted for seven years, until Deborah decided that the brand "could not foster women in the wine industry the way [she] had hoped." To extend the reach of her vision and resources, in 2015 Deborah organized the first Global Symposium of Women of the Vine & Spirits. She told me about the leap of faith this required: "The first symposium...I prayed that 250 people would show up and I wouldn't lose my shirt, that someone would buy a ticket or sponsor. We sold out at 500 people. Last symposium sold out at 750 in less than twenty-four hours." A few months after we spoke, the 2018 gathering sold out in seven hours at over $700 a ticket. It's a big deal—two-and-a-half days of networking, tasting events, lectures, and who knows what other career-altering events, featuring a veritable catalog of corporate giants and high-powered wine and spirits women.

Women of the Vine & Spirits the symposium made way for Women of the Vine & Spirits the organization. It is dedicated to "the empowerment and advancement of women in the alcohol beverage industry." What pleased Deborah so much about the *Wine Enthusiast* nomination was being recognized for the work the organization was doing, providing scholarship, mentorship, and educational opportunities to women across all sectors of the beverage business and working with large companies to develop their diversity initiatives. Beyond promoting the visibility of a handful of top women in the wine and spirits industry, Women of the Vine & Spirits has created a "collaborative community for like-minded women to encourage, support and learn from one another, speak up, thrive and become catalysts for change in their companies and the industry." Deborah mentioned that women have the tendency not to tout their own accomplishments. It was exciting to hear something as proud as "what we have organized has really created a movement, and we've been a catalyst for diversity initiatives—to women's initiatives overall—in what has traditionally been a male-dominated industry."

Women of the Vine and Spirits board members include heavyweights such as Annette Alvarez-Peters, the woman running Costco's behemoth wine and spirits division and one of the most powerful people in the booze industry. Their corporate membership is a list of basically every big-business entity in alcohol. Members span the spectrum of jobs, from farming to bottling to marketing and media, distribution, HR—the works. It's like an Ivy League alumni association for alcohol.

Women of the Vine & Spirits offers corporate membership at a few different levels, including a one for women-owned and/or operated companies. Membership "signals to employees, potential employees, and the industry at large that the organization supports gender-diverse leadership and talent development." In other words, attract better talent by being an openly better company.

Individual membership costs $150 for a year, which includes access to "education, training, mentorship, and opportunities for networking and career development." There is a free webinar program with generally useful topics such as "Delegation" and specifically useful education on labyrinthine US alcohol regulations. Hopefully one of those webinars will help improve my networking skills. Maybe Ms. Alvarez-Peters will return my messages (Annette, if you're reading this, I don't want to know where the Kirkland Signature Scotch comes from; I just want to say I admire your work).

Wine is business, but it is also a romance. Not only for its aura of opulence, or the fact that a 750ml bottle is just enough to get two people tipsy enough to splash around in a public fountain. When you dig in, everything about fermented grape juice can be downright charming. It's ancient magic: the Greeks had a god dedicated to it; the Romans liked it so much they planted vines almost everywhere they went. On family farms throughout the world's old growing areas, arable flat land was used for food, while the tougher hillside soils were planted with grapes. It was a part of the yearly cycle and the daily meal. As many growers will tell you, deep roots make for good vino. Still, there is always more to learn.

Wine info overload is one factor in the current cultural divide in winemaking and is what wine writing colossus Jancis Robinson tried to mitigate in her book *The 24-Hour Wine Expert*. The book is extremely useful as a primer; Robinson's style is plainspoken and to the point, yet still manages to convey some of the elegance and magic of the subject material. Anyone who wonders what *grand cru* actually means, or why a waiter presents you with a little taste of a newly opened bottle (spoiler alert: it's not to see if you like it), should read this book. After completing this introductory work, one can move on to Robinson's other books, such as *The Oxford Companion to Wine* or *Wine Grapes*, or read her regular columns in the *Financial Times*. I have yet to find a writer with anything negative to say about Robinson. She has implied that her job is not to preach but to report—the critic's role to a T. As she states on her website—itself a wealth of free information—regardless of which style of wine a producer appears to espouse, "I should simply be concentrating on trying to signal clearly to my readers to which camp each wine I describe belongs." In a world of vinous pundits, Robinson is Walter Cronkite.

To the left of Robinson on the spectrum of wine opinions, Alice Feiring is queen. Her books include no-nonsense titles like *The Battle for Love and Wine, Naked Wine, For the Love of Wine,* and *The Dirty Guide to Wine* (cowritten with superstar sommelier Pascaline Lepeltier, this book somehow makes bedrock and topsoil sexy). In her first book, an engrossing series of essays that should make you love wine even if you've never tasted it, wine critic Robert M. Parker, Jr., is portrayed slightly tongue-in-cheek as a bogeyman, the target of Feiring's frustration at what she saw as the increasing homogenization of wine, in pursuit of high scores from Parker's *Wine Advocate* and its ilk. Feiring's outrage was met with an army of sympathetic readers. She was, in many ways, echoing widespread concerns around the turn of the millennium about industrialization of food systems and the loss of traditional practices and small farms.

Natural wine crusaders, called "terroir jihadists" by Parker and "terroirists" by the *Wine Economist*'s Mike Veseth, are responsible for the ever-increasing number of wine shops and bars featuring these offbeat or old-fashioned bottles, made without man-made fertilizers, pesticides, fungicides, or weed killers in the vineyard and adding nothing but minimal sulfites in the cellar. Producers of these wines give up some of the control over their final product by leaving fermentation up to the microbes already present on the grapes from their environment, or "native" yeasts. This fits right in with the movements toward things like small craft beers, organic gin, and local produce. Many of the most outspoken and groundbreaking figures in this niche are women. Is this because women are more inclined to choose social and environmental stewardship over maximum profit? I'm not sure how I feel about that conclusion. It feels too easy and is probably not true. I'm more inclined to think in a business where women's very presence as innovators and entrepreneurs breaks convention, walking away from conventional techniques might be less daunting.

31

First-time women winemakers especially seem to be embracing organic or biodynamic principles at a faster rate, reflecting the greater cultural change. Elisabetta Foradori is widely credited with single-handedly reviving the near-forgotten teroldego grape of her native Trentino. Referred to by distributors as "one of Italy's superstar winemakers," Foradori's career began in 1984, at twenty years old, after her father died suddenly and she, an only child, was faced with managing the estate. Chemical and industrial farming was the norm at that time, and the Foradori estate made "perfectly fine table wine but not much else," according to Foradori in a 2011 interview. Through selective replanting for better quality over higher yields (read: better fruit, fewer bunches), incorporating organic and biodynamic principles in farming, and revolutionizing her own cellar techniques with an emphasis on the natural, she moved the Foradori wines from obscurity to a place of worldwide praise and demand. She said in 2011, "The most important thing is to be a good farmer. You need to interact with nature in order to make a wine that symbolizes a region. And to do this you have to be proud of what you do. For me this is working the right way: with respect and knowledge of your land and your roots."

Far to the south, in Sicily, Arianna Occhipinti followed many of the same principles as her winemaking role models Elisabetta Foradori, Elena Pantaleoni, and Giovanna Morganti, though few would say her path was anything but her own. Her interest piqued in 1998 at the age of sixteen, when her uncle Giusto Occhipinti of the biodynamic COS winery invited her to come help at VinItaly, Italy's largest convention of wine growers, makers, buyers, and hangers-on. Happy for the chance to skip school for four days, Arianna went along. According to Arianna, that was a turning point: "I knew nothing about wine, but it was a fantastic experience. I met a lot of people and was immediately drawn to it."

After high school, she studied viticulture and winemaking in Milan, but she found her roots in natural winemaking put her at odds with many of the lessons. Even in writing, Arianna's English is somehow full of velvet, a bit off-kilter, yet still clear and cogent. Every wine writer and seller I have spoken to seems somewhat smitten with her, and I can see why. The cadence of a passionate personality comes through even via email. Of her time at university, she wrote, "From the beginning I've been passionate of natural wines, made on principles that often went against the theories studied at the university. I certainly remember some episodes of confrontation with my professors"— rifts she believed were "right and necessary" for an eighteen-year-old to have with her elders. She added, "But I still remember [my professors] with affection and not in a negative sense."

She finished school at twenty-one and went back to Sicily to make wine her way. By twenty-three her wines drew the notice of international importers Joe Dressner and Kevin McKenna, and she became a darling of the global natural wine set.

Occhipinti wine is made from only what are known as native varietals to Sicily—frappato, nero d'Avola, albanello, and zibibbo. "When I started making wine, it was the moment when we were rediscovering in Italy...hundreds of [indigenous] grapes we have. We came from a solid twenty years of industrial enology that had standardized" many wine drinkers' palates, "as well as having planted many international grapes from the north to the south, without considering the real inclinations of the [land]." In a global wine market "awash with Pinot," as Alice Feiring puts it, these more obscure varietals send a clear statement. The best wine, for her, was the wine that thrived where it was planted and tasted like home.

As an expat from America's Rust Belt, this hits a tender note. The global trend toward seeking out local, authentic products and experiences also translates to the trend of younger residents of megacities returning to smaller communities to contribute to the local economy and culture. It is the opposite of the population loss suffered by places like my hometown of Buffalo, New York, since the 1960s. Interestingly, Buffalo and its comrades Cleveland and Detroit have experienced an uptick in local commerce from—you guessed it—the local food and drink sector (also from refugee resettlement, but that's a different book). Young people much like Arianna are proudly representing their roots around the world.

Martha Stoumen, Martha Stoumen Wines
Photo Credit: Kathryn Rummel

Having set up a vine-to-bottle winery and secured worldwide distribution before the age of thirty, Arianna reflected, "Surely I went a bit fast; I accelerated the timing and started working very early indeed, taking life very seriously and not sparing so much energy." Her father reminded her that energy is not an infinite resource, that it can be used up quickly or spread out over time. "Thirty years old was a turning point for me because I looked closely at what I had achieved...but also realized I had to slow down in some ways. From the moment when I had...a company that works, of which I was proud and with wines I was happy with, I decided to reorganize everything in order to safeguard my energy for the future."

Her primary focus remains wine, but her interests are many. She considers Occhipinti the company a broader agricultural one. "First of all I am a farmer who...should not only do monoculture but direct the company on a more complete agricultural cycle." Each year she also grows wheat and makes olive oil. For young winemakers, she suggests "research and know very well your territory and in particular the land you decide to plant to make wine." What territory does a person know better than their home state?

California winemaker Martha Stoumen's website characterizes her approach to her wines as one of patience. The patience required to farm according to organic principles, and the patience to let those wild yeasties do their thing in the cellar. Her business strategy might not seem to follow this ethos at first glance; Martha began making wine out of a shared Richmond, California, winery in 2014 and has since earned a fierce following. Her first three vintages sold out completely. Martha told me from her home in Berkeley that the consumer response to the wines took her a bit by surprise, that she "sold them faster than [she] ever imagined." She went on to clarify, however: "I did have eleven years in the wine industry to cultivate relationships. That wasn't nothing."

Eleven years feels like patience to me.

Martha is the picture of a sun-touched Northern Californian. Raised in a liberal town in Sonoma County, she did not grow up thinking she would ever settle close to home. Her initial academic interests were farming and ecology, rather than wine. After studying traditional agricultural systems and Italian in undergrad, she signed on for an internship at the Spannocchia farm in Tuscany, working the vineyards and olive orchard. It was a ground-up educational experience.

"It was more learning about agriculture systems as a whole," Martha said, "which is the angle I came at it from originally. They weren't even selling wine commercially—it was for the community and the people that worked on the farm."

From there, she came back to California with an interest in wine but little to no winemaking experience. Back in Sonoma, she "started working at a place called Chalk Hill, which compared to the Italian farm was the complete opposite." That is, an internationally renowned commercial winery that carries its own appellation. "It was very structured, it was a commercial business, but still, I learned there about native fermentations. Chalk Hill's thing was making rich California chardonnay, but it was interesting because they were doing native fermentations. I learned how amazing chardonnay lees are—the sediment in chardonnay is like the bones when you're making a broth, it brings out amazing characteristics in wine.

"After that I went to Germany. At this point I still knew so little about winemaking, I basically would drink something and be like, 'Oh, this German Riesling is delicious. Let me talk to people to find out who I should learn from.'" This led her to the Heymann-Löwenstein vineyard in the Mosel, the iconic German valley known for producing bright, lemony Rieslings from rocky slate soil. "I worked mostly in the vineyard. It was all on these steep, slate-terraced vineyards that were originally built by the Romans. If you ever want to get in extremely good shape, you should go work in the Mosel, because it was like climbing Machu Picchu every morning...I could not eat enough butter."

At this point I still knew
so little about winemaking,
I basically would drink something and be like 'Oh, this
German Riesling is delicious.
Let me talk to people to find
out who I should learn from.'

After her time scrambling up and down hillsides in Germany, Martha came back, once again, to California. This time she enrolled in a master's program at UC Davis. I wondered how the enology curriculum suited her, with her background in organic viticulture and native yeast fermentation, but she had a definite positive view of the experience.

"By the time I got to Davis I had a pretty clear concept of what I wanted to learn in terms of winemaking. It was more or less 'what's the microbiology of wine?' 'How is it working when we're not intervening?' I got a lot of information on that," she recalls. On those corrective cellar techniques: "The stuff that I didn't really care to learn, I kind of didn't. Which is I guess the point in grad school, is that you should know what you want to learn and what you don't."

After completing a master's at Davis, Martha began thinking about resettling back near her roots in NorCal. Taking a more targeted approach to her work, she took jobs at COS winery in Sicily (run by Giusto Occhipinti, Arianna's uncle) and then Didier Barral in the South of France. Both these areas have warm coastal climates similar to Martha's Sonoma home and both wineries offered important insights on traditions.

Having learned winemaking in four countries, on two continents and one island, Martha brought all her acquired technique to her vintages. Returning to California, she began finding growers—that is, vineyards that sell their grapes to wineries—mostly through word of mouth. She focused on Mendocino County, north of Sonoma, home of many family-owned vineyards, many of which had been planted in the early twentieth century by Italian immigrants. I asked her if she imagined she'd be returning so close to her roots.

"I think we have these relationships with the place we grow up—good or bad—but they're very deep-seated...Most people grow up and they want to leave their small town, but my end goal [became] to end up in Sonoma...or Mendocino, a very similar area. I'm going to spend twenty to forty years trying to get back there. It's a lovely long-term homecoming, I think."

Relationships are vital to a winemaker as hands-on as she is: "I go visit the farmers a lot. I'm curious how the season is going all the way through, up until harvest. I don't just go up right before harvest," as some winemakers do. "I feel like it better informs my winemaking decisions." Land in California is expensive, and for a fledgling winemaker, leasing is more practical. Martha leased one small vineyard, where she could control what was planted and how it was handled. "There [were] some existing vines there which I was really interested in, some nero d'Avola, negroamaro, a little bit of petite sirah," grapes mostly grown in Sicily, Italy, and California, respectively. She planted some more nero d'Avolaa. She liked it there.

Martha makes her wines in Richmond, just north of Berkeley, in a shared winery space. It is "just gorgeous. It's really close to the water . . . really good for fermentation and keeping things cool." She went on to add that Richmond was the site of the nation's largest pre-Prohibition winery. I felt the sense of lost history I always feel when talking about America and Prohibition, which I have come to think of as the Great Disruptor of drinks history. She laughs and adds, "One of the first things I outline for people is that they think California doesn't have that much of a history in winemaking, they think it's like 1970s onward. We're not Burgundian monks, but there is a *little* bit of history here."

Martha built her business around a few central tenets: "I basically started out with a philosophy that I wanted to use organic fruit and I wanted to make natural wine, and what were the best ways to do it. That is what brought me to Mendocino, because it's dry and easy to grow organically." Dry climates dissuade mold growth, a dire enemy of the winemaker and one that has many wet-climate growers using commercial antifungal sprays. The sprays may save the grapes from harmful microbes, but they can also kill off the native yeasts and bacteria that are essential to wild fermentation. *No bueno.*

I ask what harvest time, typically the most hectic time of year for winemakers, looks like for her as a one-person operation.

"I rent a giant flatbed and drive five tons of fruit at a time. I go up for the pick, and I'm there sorting in the vineyard and help manage the pick a bit, then I drive the fruit down to [the winery]. That is a space I share with four other winemakers. We are self-run, so we all do our own winemaking. We don't have a hired crew or anything. Once I truck the grapes down I decide what to do with them. That might mean me jumping in and foot-treading them. All of the work involved with the winemaking, which lasts about three months usually. Then I decide how to age the wines and do all the work involved with that as well, up until bottling." While she mentioned she might be able to take on an intern in 2018, at the time of this writing she does all of that by herself.

What goes into the bottles depends on the grapes, and Martha often doesn't know exactly which wines she'll be putting out until this point. She tells me an anecdote:

"The vineyard that I leased, we were going through a pretty intense heat wave this fall—up in the Ukiah area it was between 100 and 110 for two straight weeks. This area, I dry-farm it, I don't irrigate it, so I don't have the option to give the vines water in hard times. What happened was basically the vines' metabolism just stopped, because they were just too stressed out. So the acidity ended up being really, really high on these grapes. So when I brought them back to the winery, instead of making red out of them like I usually do, I made a little bit of red, which I know I'll need to age longer to wait for the acidity to calm down, but then I made a rosato. That was a day-of decision." She recalled her process in that moment: "I stopped for a few hours, I took a walk down to the water, and I was like, *What am I going to do with these grapes?* Then, coming back, I foot-tread them and let them sit on the skins overnight, then I made a dark rosato out of them. It's one of my favorite wines that I made. Being willing to trust your intuition is a huge thing. It's served me right." Though larger wineries with annual orders to fill certainly don't have this kind of flexibility in their business model, it seems an appropriate perk for doing all the work oneself.

"You're not always going to make right decisions, but if you give yourself time and space to think about things, even though it's quite intensely paced, just give yourself twenty minutes to take a breather and think...*I'm making wine. It's really important to me, but I'm not in surgery or anything.* Allowing yourself to breathe is a good thing."

"

My biggest challenge going into business was becoming comfortable with money. I don't know if that has to do with being a woman or where I grew up—a lot of people where I grew up didn't talk about it...

"

When I asked Martha what her toughest challenge was in starting her wine label, she did not hesitate to answer. "My biggest challenge going into business was becoming comfortable with money. I don't know if that has to do with being a woman or where I grew up—a lot of people where I grew up didn't talk about it, and they just said, 'Follow your heart and everything else will follow that.' I think that's true, but I just wouldn't [want to] have been so shy about it. I avoided conversations that had to deal with [money]. At the end of the day, it's part of the ecosystem of any business, and to be able to discuss funding options with people is hugely important. When I try to think about what is the best advice I would give to people, including women in the industry, is don't shy away from conversations. Find out the things that are more uncomfortable to you, that you're going to have to deal with, and practice talking about those things and thinking about those things. "I think when people say, 'What can we do to help promote women in business?' for me it's just like, 'Give them access to funds.' It's not a traditional thing for women to be funded, and I see that in other sectors—I see that in tech, since I live in the Bay Area. Don't be shy to break in. There's still a lot of old boys' clubs, and I do find myself talking to men generally in conversations regarding money still. It doesn't matter, it's fine—that just happens to be the environment right now. I sometimes get the feeling from people that I meet, especially growers, and it happens mostly in the older generation, but it's this sense of 'she's just *playing* at business.' I'm just as serious about this as anyone else is, and at the end of the day, having access to funding is very important."

No one I've yet encountered has defined organic, biodynamic, and "do-nothing" farming methods with as much clarity and lyricism as Deirdre Heekin does in her book *An Unlikely Vineyard.* This is probably due to her master's degree in creative writing, just one of the things she did before starting her brand, La Garagista. "Unlikely" is an apt descriptor for her career as well as the wines she makes. She and her husband, Caleb Barber, began their professional lives as artists: he was a visual artist, she a writer and filmmaker; both were dancer/choreographers. Their work took them to Italy, and an extended stay in Tuscany changed everything, as it is wont to do. Her creative channel turned from physical to culinary, and when they returned to the United States, the couple settled in Vermont and opened Osteria Pane e Salute to honor the places that awakened their senses back in Italy.

Deirdre farms organically, making "alpine wines" from cold-resistant, hybridized varietals such as Marquette, Frontenac, St. Croix, and La Crescent. These are crosses between the warmth-loving *Vitis vinifera* and native North American *Vitis riparia*, which doesn't make particularly palatable wine on its own. The hybrids combine the desired *vinifera* flavors with the native resistance to cold and local diseases.

In her writing, Deirdre makes a compelling case for wine being made "in the vineyard," by fostering the health of the topsoil to encourage the health of the vines and their microbiome, relying on native yeasts instead of commercial ones. She implores people who research the provenance of their food to do the same with their wine. This makes me recall my early wine education and the discovery that wine could be made in many different ways, with wildly variable results. Deirdre's emphasis on curiosity and education in all aspects of food and drink reinforces this feeling, along with the idea that consumers who *can* fight for ethical, healthy provenance in the food that nourishes them have little excuse not to.

Of course, Deirdre's farm offers all kinds of unexpected delights for the curious.

"We had an amazing thing happen this past year in our compost pile," she said—words I will love for the rest of my life—"where we compost all the seeds and skins that we don't use for other things. We had a spontaneous generation of vines from seed. We're going to nurse these along, because who knows what they are? They could've reverted back to wild plants or one of their *vinifera* ancestors; they could be completely new crosses of all of the above. I mean, who knows?" She told me this with palpable excitement.

The genetic diversity of the vines is an important consideration. As in tequila, grapes are frequently planted as clones, using cuttings from the "mother" plant. Plants grown from seed can be a wild card, just ask Michael Pollan. There's no way of knowing what kind of DNA mix is packed into a seed, and a good chance it might be dramatically different from its parent plant. Cloning ensures a predictable outcome. But what we gain in consistency, we lose in adaptation, as clone after clone is put in the soil and the plants become less adapted to their environments and more fragile. Hence, more chemical fertilizers, fungicides, pesticides. Using hybrid vines and experimenting with growing from seed are risks, but Deirdre said her offbeat vines give her an advantage in growing organically. They are better adjusted to this landscape and have built-in defenses to handle the cold and the mold.

It is this sense of exploration, this enthusiasm for *what else? what next?*, that led Deirdre to educate herself about wine, from designing wine lists for the osteria to embarking on her own planting. She describes a meal— bringing food and wine together at the farm—as a sensory performance with the land itself as headliner. She invokes her dance training and study of phenomenology in the cellar and in deciding which stretches of their land are best for vines. Her kind of artistry requires a certain letting go of control and simply observing. The volume of knowledge and opinion on wine out there can bewilder, but it also inspires intense passion, which in turn drives extraordinary careers.

Deirdre and Caleb are studies in boldness, in doing what feels right. It's not a stance available to all, but I'm deeply appreciative it's the path they chose.

Deirdre Heekin's Two Pieces of Advice for Vintners

"**O**bservation. Farming wine is all about observation. It's all about looking, seeing, touching, tasting, sensing what's going on in the vineyard and in the cellar. I could talk a long time about that. Observing what things are growing in and around your vines and what that's telling you about the farming you're doing. What it can tell you about what your vineyard needs.

"The other thing, particularly for wine and viticulture, is to taste wine. That's the single most important thing you can do is to educate your palate. Taste as widely as possible. Really study and train your palate. Not only is that schooling your senses, being observant during the farming process, [but] it's also training your palate to be observant of your fruit. Tasting when your fruit is absolutely ready for the work that you're going to do in the cellar.

"That's the single most important thing. I came to farming wine from the sommelier's perspective and I think it was the most important education that I had."

. . . .

Coly Den Haan, Vinovore
Photo Credit: White Oak Communications

I met Coly Den Haan—sommelier, serial entrepreneur, and badass—at her wine shop, Vinovore, in LA's Silver Lake neighborhood. I was immediately reminded of Jancis Robinson's assertion that a good wine shop is like a good bookstore. If Coly's place sold books, I'd expect to find Zadie Smith, Chimamanda Ngozi Adichie, Kelly Link, and Joan Didion on the shelves. The unpretentious space is long and narrow, with a sofa and low table in the center. A duplicate of the Zoltar fortune-telling machine from the 1988 movie *Big* greets you as you walk in. A bicycle hangs in the front window, and the bottles are displayed with handwritten descriptions in Tetris-like stacks of crates. A huge poster dominates the far wall, overlooking displays of gift sets and wine paraphernalia, adjacent to a cooler chilling select whites and bubbles.

The poster asks: WHAT KIND OF VINOVORE ARE YOU? Below the question is a chart of nine vino types, complete with illustrations of animal personalities like a Chinese zodiac. Each animal is color-coded (red lion, gold owl, etc.) and each holds the stem of a wineglass in its mouth. Each represents a different wine drinker, or at least a different wine mood.

It might take a few minutes of perusing to single out the most distinguishing aspect of the shop. Read the handwritten descriptions of the bottles for sale and something even more interesting comes to light. Vinovore exclusively stocks wines made by women (including multigender partnerships).

Vinovore opened to some fanfare in the fall of 2017, garnering attention for the lady-centric concept but also for Coly's pedigree in the LA restaurant scene. Originally from Santa Barbara, California, she has been working in restaurants most of her life and has been a driving force behind some of LA's most memorable wine and food destinations.

She speaks with a laid-back SoCal drawl, but I've learned not to be fooled by the no-worries veneer of LA restaurant veterans. They are so *chill* until service starts, then watch out. Coly began her service career as a busser as soon as she was legally able to work and worked her way up to bartender when she came to LA twenty years ago. A few years in, the California chapter of the Italian Association of Sommeliers (now called the North American Sommelier Association) hosted its training course in English for the first time at the restaurant where she was working, and her manager urged her to take it. Cost was a problem, though: "I didn't know if I wanted to do it or not, but then they offered to sponsor me. I kind of fell into it, but then I loved it."

She was intrigued by the diversity of people and experiences in the wine world. "All the preconceived notions people have about the wine business—like [it's all] old, rich, stuffy white dudes—when you actually learn about who's making the wine and how wine should be enjoyed, it really has nothing to do with all these rich guys in Beverly Hills with cigars, drinking their Napa Cabs."

This last bit made me wince a little, because I'd once been made fun of by wine bartender friends who, frustrated, offered me a Napa Cab after I'd been wishy-washy about their more complex offerings. I had no idea the connotations conveyed by the phrase "Napa Cab"—that is, a cabernet sauvignon from Napa Valley—which has become shorthand in some wine circles for what "luxury vodka" is to many cocktail bartenders. Read: "basic," "overhyped," "outdated." Yes, this is snobbery. It's a private indulgence after a long day on one's feet, wondering why you studied at all.

I told Coly this, and she laughed and footnoted: "There *are* some delicious ones."

Becoming a sommelier is an academically rigorous process, involving intense study of geography, geology, government regulations, cellar techniques, and grape genealogy; knowing these factors well enough to identify a flight of wines by taste and smell alone; and the intricate and archaic customs of wine service. I asked Coly if she had always had a studious bent. She laughed again.

"I *hated* school. I hated it. It took drinking to get me into it," she said with a half smile. Seriously, though: "I generally hated...the format of it, everything. But I really threw myself into the sommelier course. I found it really fascinating. I loved the viticulture, it was very scientific. The history. It really was a very all-encompassing course. It's not just about food pairing and tasting; it's about laws and the rich history, and where things are coming from, and I've also been super fascinated by how many varietals there are. It was a lot of fun and I took it super seriously.

"It launched me pretty quickly into my career. In the process of becoming a sommelier…this was like eleven years ago, now, I was thinking, *Wow, wine is unpretentious . . ."*

At this point, three women walked into the store. One of them sported a T-shirt with the Danzig logo underneath the word CHABLIS. They smiled as they took in the decor, and Coly greeted them warmly, asked that they please let her know if they had any questions.

Creating a more laid-back environment for enjoying wine has been a hallmark of Coly's career. In 2008, she and her partner Rachel Thomas opened the wine bar the Must in LA's still somewhat seedy fashion district.

"When I was in the [sommelier] training," she said, "I was like, 'Why are there no cool wine bars out there that are unpretentious at this time in LA?' I decided I really wanted to open a wine bar. It was right on the precipice of when wine bars were really becoming a thing, so I wanted to do something fun and cool and different."

Cool and different indeed, the Must featured "southern-inflected comfort food," including a grilled almond butter and marshmallow fluffernutter sandwich on brioche, and a "wide but accessible selection of wines from around the world." It was an immediate favorite for locals and quickly became a destination. Then: trouble.

"We had this crazy landlord dispute and we ended up losing our space. It was very sad. Then I opened another place called Perch, which is a big rooftop venue. I was one of the original owners of that." Perch is a mammoth, three-story, French-inspired space that is still a mainstay of downtown nightlife. She plowed on, and I began to get some sense of her momentum.

"I sold [Perch] and reopened the Must. Then sold that. Then I realized I didn't want to work in restaurants anymore. So I got the idea I wanted to open a retail shop, and again I went back to: How can I make a wine shop different? I wanted to make the shopping experience different. I wanted to make the decor different. Coming from a restaurant background, aesthetics are so important. I feel like wine shops don't have that same kind of philosophy [as restaurants] generally. There's definitely cute wine shops, but for the most part, to me, it's mostly like"— she waved a hand in the air—"wine, shelves. It's very utilitarian. I wanted to create something really cozy and fun. Then: How do I make the shopping experience different? And that's where the chart came in."

At this point, the three shoppers were looking at the chart intently and turned to Coly to ask about it. She explained the concept: choose the animal that describes your taste and/or mood. It lists nine color-coded wine personalities, a zodiac of tastes.

"If you're an orange tiger"—she pointed at the tiger on the chart— "look for the bottles with the orange sticker on them."

All four of us, the customers and I, let out a collective, *"Ohhhhhh."* This, to me, is the primary genius of the shop—not only this method of demystifying the selection process, but the fun of it. It's interactive. Find your "sign," find your wine by the color with which it is marked. You don't need to debate with the shop owner if this Rhône blend is *really* enough like the syrah your friend usually drinks. If your friend is a purple ape, they'll probably like the purple-stickered wine, even if it's a grape varietal they've never heard of.

The customers debated their animals. One had a platinum-blond pixie cut and mused that she might be a silver fox.

The silver fox description read:

> *An elegant tastemaker with desires of the finer things in life. A refined, sharp and sleek mind. Don't mess with a Silver Fox or chances are your invite will get lost in the mail.*
> *MOOD: Extravagant, crafty, exquisite.*
> *WINES: Fresh sparkling wine, crisp wines, briny & mineral wines.*

It's great copy. *Maybe I am a silver fox, too,* I thought. *No...a green snake. Wait...red lion. Hmm.*

"Some people are a few animals..." Coly continued, and she and her customers debated their palates. Chablis Shirt worked in wine and was visiting from out of town. Her friends *had* to bring her here. The shop is everything a progressive wine aficionada could ask for.

For Coly: "The chart was actually the original premise for the shop, before the lady winemaker thing. I was trying to think how do I make this shop different from every other shop, and this is what I came up with. Because I like to have geeky stuff, but you don't want to be intimidating. When you can walk into these 'cool' wine shops, I know what I'm doing, but you don't want people to feel like they can't try something new, or they just go for whatever is the cheapest, with the cutest label. They drink chardonnay because they know it, or merlot." Not knocking all chardonnay or merlot, per se, but it does break one's heart to see so many satisfying wines passed over because their names don't start with "pinot."

"A woman is involved in every bottle we carry," she affirmed, responding to the customers' question. They seemed pleased.

Just before the 2016 election, Coly said, "I'd already signed the lease here for Vinovore. The landlord was lagging, so I was just trying to rethink and rethink what I could do here. The election was happening and everything seemed like...all pointing to this one direction. So I started thinking: *What if I just carry female winemakers?* I started talking to my peers about it—other ladies in wine. Mainly my reps that I buy wine from. They all freaked out and were like, 'Yes, yes, yes, yes, you have to do it.' Now that's definitely our identity."

When I heard about a woman-centric wine shop in town, I was over the moon. As she pointed out, the 2016 election felt like a blow, like half the country had turned to the other half and shrugged, like, *What are ya gonna do about it?* In response, the Women's March and the #MeToo movement helped build a sense that something real and necessary was under way. Clearly, inclusivity needs to be addressed across all racial and gender identities. But for the first time that I could remember, there was widespread imperative for women to support one another openly, without apology. This public statement, *wines made by women,* applied only to a small retail shop in LA, but it felt wonderfully bold.

I asked how the neighborhood has responded to her presence.

"You just saw it," she said, gesturing toward the door, as Chablis Shirt and her friends exited with their purchases. "It's been awesome. A lot of people are just happy to have a cool wine shop in the neighborhood. A lot of people are really happy to support the female winemaker thing. Women and men alike. Men have really positive responses, too. There have actually been girls that come in saying their husbands or boyfriends have read about it and told them to come in here. Which is fun—*There's a lady wine shop, why aren't you buying wine there?* And then I've had guys whose wives tell them to come in here. It's a very interesting support system."

I noticed from the full shelves that there doesn't seem to be any shortage of wine made by women. Was it a challenge to fill them?

"No. There are a lot of great wines. I've had a lot of people that I've worked with in the past, you know, you have relationships, so when I told them what I was doing, they started digging in their book and they're like, 'I found wines that I didn't even know I had because now I'm only looking for this particular kind of wine, all the wines made by women.' It seems like it's been a fun process for my reps, too. And then I had a lot of people coming out of the woodwork that I haven't worked with in the past that are trying to sell me their lady-made wine. And I've had winemakers approach me, too, like the Nasty Woman wine, she reached out to me and she just came down from Oregon to start selling her wine. It's done really well. It's fun. Nicole Walsh is going to be down here next week, Faith Armstrong[-Foster] . . ."

There seemed to be a lot of women making amazing wine right now, at least from where I was sitting. I mentioned that I'd been trying to interview a couple of them whose wines I purchased earlier at her shop: Arianna Occhipinti and Martha Stoumen.

Coly perked up. "Have you talked to Arianna yet?...She's amazing." Note: I told you everyone loves Arianna. "She and Elisabetta Foradori.

When I met [Elisabetta] I was like, *Omigod, omigod, omigod!*" She laughed. "I totally freaked out. She was like, *Who the fuck are you?* Granted, it was the last day of RAW, she was pretty over it."

RAW is "one of the most exciting collections of fine, natural, organic and biodynamic wine artisans to regularly come together across the world," according to its website; an organization hosting four international fairs for natural wine growers to bring their precious bottles to enthusiasts, importers, and retailers. It also happens to be founded by a woman: Isabelle Legeron, author of the book *Natural Wine.*

I asked Coly if she thought there was a greater percentage of women in natural wine than in conventional wine. It's a shaky theory and I wanted an expert opinion. Coly does not say a definitive yes or no.

"One of the through lines that I've seen with female winemakers is that they tend to care more about the terroir and the grape, [using little] processing...which is the style that I like, that isn't all about varietals." She continued: "I really like to see the grape shine. Women winemakers are not looking for high alcohol, which is what California was known for, and oaking the shit out of everything and getting the most of extraction of fruit and alcohol as possible. All these wines are subtle and beautiful."

The afternoon was getting on, and a pair of men in their thirties entered the shop and started poking around. Coly engaged them, then let them browse. I asked her about an issue I'd heard from spirits producers and restaurateurs, so far, about dealing with distributors. These middlemen are frequently described as just that—men in between you and your goal. As an upstart beverage director earlier in her career, was it intimidating to deal with these suit-and-tie-wearing gatekeepers?

"I think [I felt] less intimidated and more irritated. Especially when I first got into the business. I'd go to these trade tastings and I'd feel very much ignored, talked down to. Even when I owned my own restaurant I'd have male reps come in and start telling me what wine I liked. *Oh, your customers are going to love this and you'll love this.* And I'm not one to be wearing my somm pin all the time, saying, *Don't you know who I am?* But that was really frustrating. It still happens from time to time, but

Owning your own business in and of itself is very hard. Being in wine and opening a business are two very different things. You have to have a very entrepreneurial spirit and mind and incredible determination and really thick skin.

I have finally come to a place now where it's known; people accept my understanding."

She reflected for a second and added, "I'm not even like a girlie dainty girl, either, and I still got it. I can only imagine the mega-babes in the wine industry, what they deal with."

For a moment I couldn't help imagining a *Charlie's Angels*–like gang of "mega-babes," armed with corkscrews and spit buckets. I made a mental note to suggest it as a book cover. Did her male colleagues face the same condescension?

"Of course they didn't. At Perch I decided I wanted to do an all-French wine list because we wanted to make it very Parisian...but I remember this wine rep that was like, 'I don't think that's a good idea, I mean, you're going to want to carry, like, Napa Cabs and Cakebread Chardonnay.' I said, 'No, actually, I don't.' I mean, who would tell an owner of their own restaurant that what they're doing is not a good idea? Are you crazy, dude?" At this point I'm thinking anyone who would second-guess Coly to her face would have to be a little foolhardy.

I ask her if she would do anything differently if she could.

"I'm not a person of regrets," she says, "but I've definitely had a difficult journey. Owning your own business in and of itself is very hard. Being in wine and opening a business are two very different things. You have to have a very entrepreneurial spirit and mind and incredible determination and really thick skin, especially being a woman in business. There have been been plenty of times when I've wanted to tell people to go fuck themselves when they talked down to me...but you've got to be PC. Sometimes I haven't been, and that's okay, too. So gosh, I don't know. If it's passion and it burns inside you, then go all the way and run with it."

Alice Feiring has been driving the discussion on wine and winemaking practices for more than ten years, with four books to her name and a popular subscription-based newsletter, the *Feiring Line*, which she has published since 2012. Her writing was an entry point for me into a world that I knew very little about. I knew I was drawn to certain kinds of wine and that these wines were frequently labeled "natural," "wild," or "biodynamic." They had a freshness and an unpredictable element to them that I found lacking in most of the wines I was pouring at my restaurant jobs, which seemed designed to fit neatly into the slots of the customers' expectations and nothing more. Through these wild wines, I found the books and then the author. I met Ms. Feiring on a snowy day in Manhattan, at a bookstore cafe a few blocks from the downtown flat she has described as a "fifth floor walkup with a bathtub in the kitchen," her home base since the beginning of her career.

The term "natural wine" has finally permeated mainstream culture, and I wanted to know how she felt about this. Alice expressed some ambivalence. The "Parkerization" of traditional styles had seemed to ebb, and interesting, ethically produced wine was more widely available. Still, she feared that "natural" had become a buzzword as problematic as "organic" in foods, a malleable concept, easily exploited for marketing purposes.

The mainstream absorption of the topic is a relatively recent development. Until a few years ago she was one of a very few people writing about it.

"But there's a very good reason for that," she continued. "You can't make a living. I was a whistleblower, and we know what happens to whistleblowers."

I was hoping they were rewarded handsomely and recognized for their contributions, but suspected it was not so. She had made a living, writing about natural wine, though. Right?

"No," she said, and I tried to keep from spitting out my tea. This was not what the aspiring booze writer wanted to hear.

She conceded: "I mean, pathetically. I started my newsletter as a way to make a living. For somebody who is as well-known as I am—and I have the feeling it would be different if I were a man—as well-known internationally as I am, I've never been given a platform."

Alice Feiring
Photo Credit: Andrew French

She had been quoted before as saying she was not a wine critic but a wine writer, and that difference is crucial. She does not evaluate the relative merits of a particular brand or vintage and report to the consumer. Rather, she finds wines that interest her, seeks out their birthplaces, and writes about her experiences in tasting the goods and meeting the winemakers. This narrative approach resonated with me more than any 100-point ratings scale. The wines' stories made me want to taste them, to see if I could discern the magic for myself. It was a kind of writing I'd loved from culinary essayists like M.F.K. Fisher and Kingsley Amis. After we'd settled in at the miniature round table with our cups of hot black tea, Alice remarked with an irony-laden New Yorker smile, "I never wanted to be a wine writer. If I'm going to be this poor I'm going to go back to writing."

This reminded me of a conversation I'd had with Amy Stewart, the author of *The Drunken Botanist*, which is a book every human should read. In it, Amy describes all the plants that go into making alcoholic beverages worldwide in glorious, scientific, and humorous detail. When I spoke to her, I accidentally referred to Amy as a scientist. She corrected me: she was not a scientist, not a bartender. She was a writer—she had several novels to her name in addition to her nonfiction. This was the privilege of the profession: to research and interpret, to become authorities on things we do not do for a living. The at-times deeply misogynist criticism directed at Alice from some in the wine world missed this point. She was not telling people what to drink. She was telling the story of drink.

Seeing a subject change on the horizon, I made for it with haste. I made a non sequitur into Amy Stewart's assessment of the "progress" women have made in the spirits industry in that same conversation. I had been going on about how, at a recent cocktail conference, so many women were presenters, experts, award nominees. Sure, Amy had countered, but when she was there, there were still women in bustiers and fishnet tights carrying trays of beverages around hotel lobbies. It was all objectification couched as tradition or style.

I brought this up with Alice in relation to an anecdote she mentioned in another interview, about Pascaline Lepeltier, a master somm who was credited with building the "world's best wine list" at Rouge Tomate Chelsea a few years ago. During the Best World Sommelier competition in France, one of the judges docked Pascaline for her presentation, suggesting she needed to wear some makeup, don shoes with heels, and look a bit more like a lady.

"They also told her she was too enthusiastic, that it was distracting from the wine."

I see, I thought. *Care, but not too much.* That seemed more French than sexist, actually, but the makeup bit was infuriating. Alice considered for a moment.

"There are way more [women] presenters [at cocktail / wine conventions], but who's in control and who holds the money? I think it was Pascaline... saying how hard it is for a woman to own a restaurant, because banks aren't giving money to women. The boys' club everywhere is still extremely fierce. Even though women are allowed to get up on the stage and talk, they're not necessarily the ones in charge. They're not given the money to do really great stories. They're not given that four- and five-dollar-a-word rate to actually go and do a really good wine story. It does help if you went to Princeton or Yale and you have access to the club in that way. That's also part of it, too, the privileged class—you can kind of circumvent the barriers. It's complicated. It's never any one thing."

I suggested that it was not only privilege at play, but also how many women, in my experience, were not raised to talk about money, to ask for it, or to negotiate. Alice nodded: that was hard, she agreed.

"Asking is tough," Alice said. "I remember the first time I was asked to give a talk. It was for Sud de France or something. The guy that usually did it couldn't, and he passed it over to me. I don't understand corporate America, and back then I had absolutely no idea."

She'd rationalized: "It was in town, I just needed to get up and talk with very little preparation. They were going to sell my book... I had to spend about an hour and a half there. This was about eight years ago; I charged $300. I talked to him afterward, he said, 'They told me what you asked for, and you've got to stop that. That's completely embarrassing.'

That made me feel like shit. He could've offered me advice on what to ask for. Women always do this for one another. I was thinking, 'How much the fuck did you get paid?'" She rolled her eyes and added, "He had nowhere the kind of experience that I had."

Setting my own pay rate is a constant source of anxiety as a freelancer. Every time I'm asked what my rate is, there's that soft, motherly voice in my head that warns me not to be presumptuous. We just want so much to be liked.

I wanted to ask her about mentorship. In *The Battle for Wine and Love*, Alice wrote affectionately about her professional relationship with importer Joe Dressner of New York's Louis/Dressner. "Big Joe" and his Burgundian wife, Denyse Louis, founded the operation in the 1980s, seeking out low-intervention wines well before anyone was talking about natural wine. If Joe helped her learn about was there anyone who helped her in publishing?

"I never had a mentor. I always wanted one but never had one. Actually back then, the wine writing community was far more welcoming than it is now. [Executive director of the Wine & Spirits Education Trust] Mary Ewing-Mulligan was very kind about wine tasting and reached out to offer me a couple classes that she was giving at the WSET. But it was odd, because I never really wanted to be a wine expert." I did an internal double take at this. "I've had mentors but not in the wine writing world. Becky Wasserman [founder of Becky Wasserman & Co. wine distributors], who helped me understand Burgundy on a deeper level. But as far as wine writing, I just fumbled my way through it."

Perhaps this was how she maintained her autonomy and singular voice, not being indoctrinated into one style of criticism or another, I posited.

"When I kept on showing up in Europe they realized I was serious. What made a big difference was the publication of *The Battle for Wine and Love* in French; it made a huge difference with the French winemakers. They realized I was independent...I was coming alone."

Showing up without an agenda surely implied integrity.

When I kept showing up in Europe they realized I was serious... The French [said] that they understood the life of a writer is difficult, but I had my freedom. My opinion wasn't being bought.

"Integrity and freedom. The French kept on saying that they understood the life of a writer is difficult, but I had my freedom. My opinion wasn't being bought. Everybody in France's opinion is bought, too, it's not just America."

Because I couldn't help it, I added that freedom must feel even nicer if you have state health care. At this, she laughed.

"That's what I said."

This topic seemed to spur warmer feelings than talking about misogyny in publishing. It was clear that Alice wrote about people and things that fascinated her, through the lens of an indomitable progressive ethical code. This was why she'd operated independently, and why, in her own words, no one gave her a larger platform.

If it wasn't all for the gobs of cash, what were some of best experiences this career had afforded her?

At this, Alice grinned again. "Certainly all of the times that I've gone to López de Heredia. Clos Roche Blanche, Domaine Romanée Conti…" I tried to keep up amid the coffee shop's din. She spoke of little towns in Italy's Alto Piemonte, mentioned Elisabetta Foradori, traveling to the Canary Islands. She was talking about some of my favorite passages from her books. She listed off a few more names that neither my novice ears nor my recorder caught, the pleasure of her nostalgia starting to show.

"Oh, my god! Bartolo Moscarello! Nobody's ever asked me this. You know, I got to catch a lot of people before they disappeared."

Were there traditions she saw in action that have since disappeared?

"I think I got to see the last of the traditional Châteauneuf[-du-Pape]. The area has absolutely no interest for me anymore, because it got Parkerized and stayed Parkerized. The old style of working with grenache is mostly gone. It's one flavor that I never get in wine anymore." She was less vexed by this than I imagined from having read her early work. It came out why: "But now, I think now, except for the Châteauneuf, and that'll happen, too…they're coming back. Wine is cycling back and readjusting. So that's great."

Wine is cycling back, I thought. Does that mean Alice's battle is won? When she began writing about it, it seemed that all wine would eventually become homogenized—big, red, fruity, and oaked to the teeth. Alice's work helped spark the countermovement and bring wine into the discussion of where our food comes from and how it is processed. Despite commercialism co-opting the label, natural wine as a movement has succeeded in keeping conversations of biological, regional, and technical diversity going. Biodynamic methods and sustainability are taken seriously, and there are wine bars popping up all over the country dedicated to Alice's kinds of wine.

I told her that when I read her story about her life-changing glass of Barolo from her father's mistress's wine cellar, it set off a lightbulb for me about my own gateway wine. It was from a California producer: La Clarine Farm's Jambalaia Rouge. This wine was a chilled, light-bodied red that made my soul perk up, gave me the first notion that there might just be something to this wine-tasting stuff beyond a buzz and free baguette. It was fresh and delicious and biting and nothing like any kind of wine I'd had before.

Alice nodded knowingly. She was familiar with the vintage; she said, "It's wild," and that she'd "have to write to Hank and tell him that. It'll put a smile on his face."

Women. Beer. Professionals.

Craft beer in America has always been essentially DIY. Despite today's stories of multimillion-dollar company sales to corporate beverage behemoths, if you plumb the histories of most of North America's independent breweries, you will find a couple of people cooking up mash in their kitchen. Such humble origins are central to craft brewing's identity, like plaid shirts, IPAs, and—problematically—being populated almost entirely by white dudes.

Women making and enjoying beer is no new phenomenon. The ancient Sumerians—you know, the world's first known urbanized civilization—had a goddess of brewing by the name of Ninkasi. The hymn sung in her honor is considered the first written recipe for beer making. Fred Minnick gives a great account of women's involvement in brewing in his book *Whiskey Women*, since brewing is the first step in making whiskey. Likewise, the Pink Boots Society historian Tara Nurin writes extensively on the history of women and beer, from Sumer to ancient Egypt, from brewsters in medieval Europe to early American household brewers and beyond.

So what happened? Somewhere along the line, beer became more than another household foodstuff you drank because the water was full of

Teri Fahrendorf, Pink Boots Society
Photo Courtesy of Pink Boots Society

parasites. According to Nurin, by the 1700s, brewing had become a big enough capitalist venture for the people in charge (i.e., dudes) to push women out of the game, supposedly using some handy anti-witchcraft propaganda to do so. A woman over a kettle meant loss of profit to a male brewer, and it was possibly too easy to equate the bubbling of mash with a little *double, double, toil and trouble.* This shutout persisted in the ensuing centuries, up through the post-Prohibition era in the United States that saw drastic consolidation in the beer industry and the meteoric rise of mass-produced, commercial lagers. Beer was big business, no place for a lady in the '50s and '60s (and somehow not much through the '70s and '80s, either).

The growing popularity of "craft"—different styles of beer made in smaller batches, in smaller facilities by small-business people—seemed a perfect opportunity for women to regain their former status in brewing. The aforementioned DIY ethic and focus on quality over quantity seemed absolutely ripe for a more gender-balanced industry, more meritocratic and less stratified in its ranks. Yet until recently, the number of women brewmasters has been microscopic, the total percentage of women-owned breweries even smaller. The industry's gender imbalance was so severe that for years, many women brewers thought they might be all alone.

This was the case as recently as 2007, when Teri Fahrendorf became the Road Brewer. What started out as one person's road trip to brew beer with her friends and visit family turned into an online phenomenon and helped launch one of the most important organizations of beer professionals in the world. At the time, Teri told me, she was just ready to do something new.

She had been a brewmaster for nineteen years, seventeen of those at Steelhead Brewing in Eugene, Oregon: "I was hired before [Steelhead] opened, and I helped build it to what it became, so I was really proud of it." She knew it was time to go do something else, but "wasn't quite ready to fall in love with another company."

Teri grew up loving beer. To her German family in Wisconsin, beer was part of the culture and daily life, and Teri and her siblings have imbibed (moderately) since childhood. Legend has it Teri found a pamphlet titled *How to Brew Beer* at a church rummage sale when she was nine and became sorely disappointed when she and her sister learned the process involved so much heavy equipment. By ten, her fermentation fervor brought her to making bread; at nineteen, she was making homemade wine for her college roommates. Experiments in winemaking continued through her college years, increasing in breadth and complexity. Upon moving to San Francisco after graduation, a place where "decent wine could be had so cheaply," she and her then boyfriend moved on to home-brewing beer. That was 1984. Four years later she became the first female master brewer west of the Rockies.

Running the show at Steelhead for so long had been a wellspring of new experiences. Not the least of these was meeting other brewmasters. "I had a lot of peers, but my peers didn't work with me at the same company. They were from all over the country," Teri told me over the phone from her office at Great Western Malting, a company that supplies brewing and food materials all over the United States and Canada. She had a thought: "It would be amazing somehow if I could go brew with people. Put on the boots—they were black boots back in those days—and go brew with... my brewing friends, because it's one thing to taste their beer like at the Great American Beer Festival and it's like, 'Oh, it tastes like this,' but the question with brewers is...your beers are your children; how are your children behaving when they're away from home?"

Teri speaks at a pace and with as much enthusiasm as you would expect from someone who could build three or four different careers amid a haze of boiling mash. I was happy to have my recorder on. Even though she professed to being tired, she ran circles around me.

"Then a lot of my relatives were in their eighties, and I thought, *Geez, these aunts and uncles are not going to live a lot longer,* so I thought, *I'll visit my aunts and uncles and my husband's relatives as well.*" In 2007, her road trip began to take shape as Teri "connected the dots" between relatives and brewer friends, and made detailed plans to maintain her budget, hygiene, and sanity.

"I would try to hit certain events"— on her way home, she would judge at the Great American Beer Fest, for one—"but there were still sections of the country where I didn't have any landing spots. I was in a Chevy Astro minivan towing a what was called a Fun Finder camper made by Cruiser RV. The maximum length was fifteen feet, and mine was like fourteen feet, nine inches." There was room to sleep and eat, and a toilet, but no shower. The rig came in at just under thirty feet.

"I had to arrange camping spots, and then every other day I wanted to shower. So [I'd call people and say] 'Hey, you don't know me, but . . .' "

The trip was plotted out: 139 days, from June 4 to November 3, 2007, from Eugene, Oregon, to Bar Harbor, Maine, and back. Five months on the road while unemployed. "I put the word out on the brewers' forum and said, 'Hey, if you want me to visit your brewery, drop me an email.' So people I did not know would start inviting me. I put in [the forum post]: 'And I need a place to park. It's thirty feet long, and if you got a place for me to take a shower, that would be awesome.'"

She would park in "crazy places." Sometimes brewers insisted she stay in their children's bedrooms and made her breakfast. Some brought her to see special local events—the sunset over the bay off the hook of Cape Cod, for instance. Teri did not have time for sightseeing, mostly, but, she said, "people were just so kind."

Teri developed a routine: "Wake up in the morning at a brewery in their parking lot, go in, brew with them until lunchtime, and if it's a brewpub, hopefully they'll buy me lunch because I'm unemployed. Then, in the afternoons, blog about it and then get in the van and tow the camper to the next place. I'd try to get there before dinner, because if it's a brewpub, maybe they'll want to buy me dinner."

I wonder at some point in our conversation how a person acquires the amount of chutzpah I imagine it takes to hop from town to town requesting showers. Teri answered me without being asked. She'd been pretty much the only woman in her workplace for almost two decades.

"I built five breweries for Steelhead. I'd walk down the construction site and the construction guys were like, 'Hey, little lady, are you lost?' I'd

"

I built five breweries for Steelhead. I'd walk down the construction site and the construction guys were like, 'Hey, little lady are you lost?' I'd put on my big-boy voice and I'd go, 'I'm your brewmaster and I'm going to be working with you guys for the next three months.'

"

put on my big-boy voice and I'd go, 'I'm your brewmaster and I'm going to be working with you guys for the next three months.' They got used to me. What happens [with male brewers] is that first of all, it's 'Who's this chick?' and then I'd open my mouth and they'd be like, 'Oh, she's okay.' Then we'd start talking beer buzzwords as if it's with other brewers, and the next thing you know: I'm just a brewer."

Still, she felt a responsibility in this to be more than "one of the guys." There were so few women working in the field at that time that Teri knew she might be the first woman brewer most of them had ever seen. She had to represent.

"So I said, 'I'm really representing my gender. It's very easy for me to just become one of the guys because we just talk beer stuff.' She mentioned to her husband that she wished she had a pair of pink rubber boots, like the black boots brewers wear to keep their feet dry in the messy business of brewing. The footwear spoke to her competence and experience, and the color was a reminder that femininity and beer were not mutually exclusive. The thought passed, as pink rubber boots were not to be found just lying around, especially in the throes of planning an expedition. Just before she left, though, "this box came in the mail from my mother-in-law. There was a pair of pink rubber boots. I went on the brewers' forum and I said, 'Hey, everybody. I'm going to be coming in a pair of pink rubber boots.'"

Wearing her pink boots city to city and brewery to brewery on her tour in 2007, Teri undertook her plan to park, brew, shower, and move on. Her friends back home had demanded email updates along the way, but she was not about to spend her evenings sending batches of emails, so she started a blog. It was the first blog she'd ever attempted. She called it the *Road Brewer* blog—still readable at roadbrewer.blogspot.com. I can't help making *Mad Max* connections, and it's oddly fitting. Teri is tough.

Not too far into the trip, in San Marcos, California, Teri found out she was part of something bigger.

"I was there at Port Brewing, which is the Lost Abbey brewery, working with the owner and the assistant brewer. I was bottling at this little hand bottler, wearing my pink boots, and this guy comes in and he says, 'Oh my god. You're the pink boots lady.' He said, 'I was just reading your blog yesterday.'"

The Road Brewer road trip had became the Pink Boots tour, and beer fans all over the world followed Teri's progress. Then something wonderful happened in San Diego. She came to Stone Brewing and was told she'd be working with Laura.

"I'm like, 'Laura? I never heard of a Laura! I didn't know you had a woman. Oh my god,'" she related her shock, laughing. "There were so few of us."

Laura was Laura Ulrich, who had recently moved to San Diego from Fort Collins, Colorado, and had been working in breweries for three years. According to Laura, who was then in her mid-twenties, she had just been promoted to the brewhouse at Stone and was trying to learn as much as she could on the job. Unlike Teri, who had been practically raised on malt and hops, Laura came to beer as a young adult, working at a punk rock bar in Fort Collins that happened to carry the few craft brews on tap.

Laura told me that when she first started, around fifteen years ago, "there wasn't a whole lot of craft beer. These guys would come around who cleaned the beer lines for Odell [Brewing Company] or New Belgium, and I thought that was just very cool. I thought what they were doing was rad. I got into beer, started drinking Odell," and when the brewery had a bottling line position open up, she went for it. She had no qualms quitting her customer service job; she was "sick of dealing with people." No arguments there.

The bottling line was a challenge. After Laura's interview, her potential boss put her on the line to see if she could do the job. "I'm five-two, I'm not super tall. They were hand-packing [the bottles]—think Laverne and Shirley. I wasn't very good at it. The manager at the time kept stressing 'the job is tough, the job is tough,' and I was like, 'This is a challenge. If you're going to give me the job, I'll take it.'"

This ready work ethic and willingness to dive into new environments would prove real assets in the field. A passion for the beer itself was still a

Laura Ulrich, Stone Brewing
Photo Courtesy of Stone Brewing

The manager at the time kept stressing 'the job is tough, the job is tough,' and I was like: this is a challenge. If you're going to give me the job, I'll take it.

little way off. She was enjoying the "cool" factor of working at a brewery—buying home-brew books for her brother, who got her into beer, but not herself—and thinking about a change of scenery. Stone Brewing had an opening, and San Diego sounded nice.

Her real affection for brewing kicked in at this job. Eventually. "All the guys were like, 'Do you home brew? Who's your favorite brewer?' and I was like, *Oh my god, I have no idea.* I thought I was just working the bottling line!" Soon enough, though, her interest was piqued: "As I started working at Stone Brewing, I was learning more and more. I saw all the equipment they had and I'm like, 'I want to learn that.' They kept trying to push me into the brewhouse and I was like, 'No, I need to learn the cellar and I need to learn all this other stuff.'" She had finally begun brewing when Teri came through San Diego in her pink rubber boots.

"I think that's when it kind of clicked in," Laura said of meeting Teri, who had nearly twenty years of professional brewing behind her. "I was like, *This is actually something that people do for a career. What am I missing? What do I need to do? How do I meet more women? Why don't I know about other women?"*

The two worked all day together, Laura peppering Teri with questions. "I could see the gears in her head spinning," Teri told me. "She's asking me a million questions because she's been in the industry about two, three years, and I've been in it for nineteen years." The workday ended, and they decided to get a beer. When Laura asked Teri if she had dinner plans, she reported she would be "camping in your parking lot, having a granola bar for dinner 'cause I'm unemployed."

Laura took her new friend to dinner at a nearby bistro, building to a question she'd been wondering since the day began. Teri was the first other woman working in beer she'd ever met. She asked, "How many of us are there?"

Teri didn't know. But she was in a good position to find out. "That was the day that the Pink Boots Society was born. It didn't have a name yet, but that was the day it started, because I just felt this strong urge to mentor her. I felt like a mother hen and my little mother hen wings came out."

After that, Teri's trip had another mission. She would visit breweries, make beer, write her *Road Brewer* blog, and keep a list of all the women brewers she could find. "I [was] just dropping names. Laura Ulrich, who else? Carol Stoudt in Pennsylvania. Who else do I know?" Carol Stoudt, for good measure, is the founder of Stoudts Brewing Company, who in 1987 became the second female craft brewmaster in the United States. The first, according to Teri and a few beer blogs, was Mellie Pullman of Schirf Brewing (now Wasatch Brewery) in Park City, Utah, in 1986. Teri, the third, she claims, earned the brewmaster title in 1988. Fast-forward to this fortuitous meeting in 2007—over two decades of massive growth for the beer industry later, and women brewers were still left feeling alone in the field.

Teri was on the case. She narrated the story to me as lively as a movie montage: "Every time I visited a brewery I'd ask, 'Do you know any women brewers?' Yes, no, maybe." Sometimes there was none. Sometimes the reference was vague: "Oh, there's one in Indiana!" She wrote down each tip. When she reached Indiana, she asked again. Some "I don't knows," some nos. "Oh, wait," she'd hear, "there's one in Bloomington." What was her name? They didn't know. Teri asked in Bloomington: "Oh, that's Eileen Martin [at Upland Brewing Company]." Teri went to find her, add her to the list, let her know she wasn't alone.

Soon another pattern emerged.

"A lot of breweries started to invite me actually because they had women employed there. There were these young women who felt all alone. One of them who is now in the malt sales field, she was a brewer at Troegs. Her name was Whitney Thompson." This was all the way in Pennsylvania, a good three thousand plus miles of road brewing since she met Laura Ulrich in San Diego. Whitney asked what Teri was doing for dinner and, after hearing the granola-bar-in-the-parking-lot plan, invited her out to dine on the boss's credit card.

How many of us are there? It became the eternal question. But by this time, Teri had a list. "There's sixty!" she told her. "Sixty in the whole world, isn't that amazing?"

Whitney wanted to know who all these women brewers were. She wanted to network, to commiserate. Teri put the list of women brewers up on her new website and named it the Pink Boots Society. People had come to know her as the pink boots lady, so she thought, *What's that group of old ladies that like to party? The Red Hat Society. I'll call it the Pink Boots Society.*

Very quickly, beer bloggers found the list and linked and reposted. Teri began to get inquiries from women around the country: The packaging manager at Bell's Brewery wanted to join. The lab manager at another place—could she join? How about a woman beer writer? "I was like...Shit, I didn't know this was something you could join!" She told the Pink Boots hopefuls that she would get back to them.

After 139 days, Teri returned to Oregon, having visited seventy-one breweries, brewed at thirty-eight, distilled at three distilleries, and blogged the entire journey. Her husband had found a new job in the meantime and a house for them in Portland. Settling into their new place, Teri realized spring was upon them, and it was almost time for the Craft Brewers Conference in San Diego.

Laura Ulrich, Teri Fahrendorf, and brewer Jessica Gilman organized the first meeting of the Pink Boots Society, which took place as a lunch for the women on Teri's list at the 2008 conference. Twenty-two women attended, sixteen brewers and six beer writers. Most wore a little pink, many brought beer to swap. "They were just yakking," Teri recalls, "they were so excited. They'd never talked to another woman brewer before." Though they had shown up for what was ostensibly a networking lunch, Teri had other plans.

"I said, 'Well, I'm glad you're having fun meeting and trying each other's beers. We're going to do some voting today.'" The question was: What is the Pink Boots Society? In addition to the brewers on the original list, Teri had invited women in packaging, who worked in labs and in the media, all of whom had asked to join. Their job that day was to decide what this organization was and who could take part.

After the debate was done, Teri "was really proud of [the brewers] for the way they came together" to decide what this new group stood for. It boiled down to three things: women beer professionals. "You must be a woman. It is not wine, it is not spirits, it's not cider; it is beer and you have to earn an income from it."

The income part was a bit contentious at first. Women approached Teri, who was by then the president, with complaints. Women who volunteered at their boyfriends' breweries doing social media or filling kegs, who taught home-brew classes from their homes for free. Why couldn't they join?

Teri held firm. For the social media volunteer: "How many tweets do you do a month?" The woman estimated around two hundred. Teri responded, "Charge a buck a tweet. Buck a tweet for the first fifty every month," then, as a social media professional, she could join. For the volunteer teacher, she asked if all those people in her community learning home brewing from her would pay ten dollars per class. That didn't seem like too much. She was also studying to become a certified Cicerone, a professional tasting/service expert—the beer community equivalent to a sommelier (more or less). The course and exam are not cheap. "That needs to pay you back," Teri told her. "You go to three local restaurants that don't have beer menus and you say, 'I got a proposal for you. If I design a beer menu for you with recommended pairings for free, will you give me a great recommendation?' After that, you charge," and so on. This was purposeful.

"The way I see it is that women have been the backbone of volunteers throughout the centuries. This world would not work without women volunteers." She brought up child-rearing and domestic work, for one. "The thing is, because of that cult of conditioning, women are quick to volunteer but slow to ask for money. It is time for women to take their place, because in our culture your worth is only considered as valuable if somebody can put a number on it."

This was a powerful climax to this long, winding story, but it rang crystal clear. She sent it home: "You've got to earn your professionalism in the way that our culture understands it, and that is your income." Teri had hit me with the meaning of it all. By forcing skilled, enthusiastic women

This world would not work without women volunteers. The thing is, because of that cult of conditioning, women are quick to volunteer, but slow to ask for money. It is time for women to take their place, because in our culture your worth is only considered as valuable if somebody can put a number on it.

in the brewing community to earn income from their work in order to join, the Pink Boots Society was helping them remove an obstacle we hear about time and time again—timidity in asking for compensation worthy of our work.

Since 2007, the Pink Boots Society has grown into a global organization, with chapters as far flung as Australia, Spain, and Hong Kong. It is a volunteer group, currently led nationally by Laura Ulrich as president. Its stated mission is "to assist, inspire and encourage women beer industry professionals to advance their careers through education." This includes providing seminars and raising money for scholarships for beer education for women. According to Laura, "The one thing we thought was lacking that would help women advance their careers was education." A few years after its inception, Pink Boots gained its nonprofit status, which allowed it to reach out to places offering classes— universities, individuals, and organizations—to offer full scholarships to women who applied through the Pink Boots website to continue their brewing education. Since 2013, Pink Boots has increased its scholarship awards from an initial six places up to between twelve and twenty-four for a given year, for things like the online Cicerone course, technical brewing courses from Siebel Institute, and online and in-person classes at Portland State University. There is a scholarship for a San Diego State University course in beer distribution, which I hear could use a few more women.

Another initiative Laura mentioned was an ongoing effort to work with the Brewers Association nonprofit to procure a "kind of a Nielsen report of how many women actually work in the industry and what roles they carry inside that industry." There exists very little hard data on this, and much of the Pink Boots Society's efforts are based on anecdotal figures and its own membership. This should inform its programming going forward. The ultimate goal of the organization, she points out, is to see its own obsolescence: "Hopefully, we won't have to have a Pink Boots Society because there's going to be a fifty-fifty split with how many women are in the industry."

Laura has been with Stone Brewing in Escondido, California, for more than fourteen years. She has been working in Stone's small-batch department for the past seven years, part of a team of five who produce the craft behemoth's "smaller-volume items." They are the research and development arm of the brewery, working on pilot projects as well as Stone's barrel and cask programs. She enjoys her job: "Once you're in it, it's a whole lot of fun to do this. I don't sit at a desk—well, occasionally—but I don't sit in a cubicle and hate my job every day. It's fun, it's unique, it's different." I ask her what education she had to wind up here.

"I have a degree in English with an emphasis in writing. I wanted to be a writer, but then I had a professor tell me that I was awful at writing, and I was like, 'Well, fuck it, I'm not going to be a writer, I'm done.'" This was not what I expected, but then again, the winding career path was thus far the norm when talking about booze jobs. She went on: "I was more interested in being done with college in four years. I think that was ultimately my goal. I didn't really care what I had to do, but I was like, 'Okay, four years, I'm done. I guess I'm not going to be a writer—I'll find something else.' I don't have the math background; I don't have the science background."

This was something I'd wondered about, since so many English majors like myself had found their way to the beer, wine, and spirits jobs via restaurant work. Is it more important now to have a solid foundation in, say, chemistry or engineering?

Laura admitted that this kind of education will make a better brewer but also added, "I think it's split. I think you have people who don't have the chemistry or the engineering or any of that stuff behind them. I'm probably not the best technical brewer, but I definitely know how to make beer. I think there's definitely two worlds to that. Some people are really good at making beer on paper, and some are really good at making beer just because of habit and knowledge and the feel, the touch, and the love."

Love was a key ingredient in kicking off Rachael Akin's beer career. She co-owns San Diego's Benchmark Brewing with her husband, Matt, and until recently with her in-laws, Jim and Margaret. Matt has been brewing beer since the day he turned twenty-one, and his passion spread to the whole family. A business does not thrive on beer alone, though.

"We like to say that [Matt] does everything inside the can, and I do everything outside it." Rachael's current title is "brand czar," which she admitted is "kind of goofy, but was the only thing [they] could come up with that encompassed everything [she does]." She pointed out that large corporations have that title, and though their five-year-old brewery is far from, say, Louis Vuitton, she feels the implications are appropriate. That is: "making sure that every single customer contact with Benchmark is seamless and similar and reinforces what we stand for and what we want to do in the beer space."

Benchmark's credo is that it makes "beer flavored beer": lower-alcohol brews across a range of five styles in its core line with no fruit or sweet flavors added. "[A beer] doesn't have to be a special occasion thing," Rachael told me, "it could just be part of your day. We want you to be able to have a beer on a Tuesday. We like doing that, too."

Like Laura Ulrich, Rachael came from an educational background in the humanities and had little interest in brewing until she found herself working at a brewery. Her training was in theater management and interior design, both of which she practiced professionally for a number of years until Benchmark opened. A previous job had entailed designing hospital interiors to be more intuitive. For example, "there [were] corridors that looked really inviting and others that looked very clinical, and it gives you that subconscious cue not to turn left." She took the same "comforting" approach to Benchmark's tasting room, "which includes everything from commissioned artwork and art tiles in bathrooms and a really patient-experience design." She reveled in the knowledge that she would "never have to hand the keys over" to anyone else. "It's just so neat to be able to grow with it and direct, design, and evolve, rather than watching someone take whatever we left them with and do what they want with it."

I enjoyed Rachael's story, not only because it demonstrates other ways to be involved in beer than in the brewhouse, but also as another example of how winding and unexpected a career path can be. Rachael admitted that even growing up in a major beer mecca like San Diego, she never imagined making beer for a living. She enjoyed drinking it and even got her certification as a certified beer judge (a program similar to Cicerone that involves rigorous study and testing to evaluate and speak on different beers) before she was involved with the industry professionally. I asked her if she'd met with any bias in the Beer Judge Certification Program, and her answer surprised me a little. Though she was one of only three women in the course, "Peter Zien, who owns and runs AleSmith, was leading the class. He often said that...women are more articulate about flavors." Note: not that women's palates are better, which I have heard debunked, but that we may be better at coming up with the words for what we are tasting, a key skill in the role of beer judge or sommelier. "Matt says regularly that I am a better judge than he is. I don't know that, but we drink a lot of beer together and I definitely find things that he doesn't notice or key in on." She added that there is "a lot more room for women in judging."

Which leads into the next surprise: when I asked if there was any truth to the craft industry's reputation as a "bro" culture, she told me that had not been her experience, at least in the five years she'd been working in it. "I've been around [the beer industry] for longer than I've been in it," she said. "People are welcoming for the most part. I would say a lot more of the discrimination comes from the customer side." Although she is co-owner of a brewery and a certified expert, when standing at her bar next to a male volunteer, she finds many customers still deferring to him. "I may know everything I know about beer and have this volunteer who just likes to drink next to me," she said with a laugh, "and whoever is walking up looks to the guy to get the answer. That's the frustrating part to me. I don't get a lot of that inside the industry. I think that people are generally encouraging and respectful and don't look at women in the industry as something that is unusual, necessarily." Granted, San Diego's brewing scene is one of the most established in the country, but this does echo Teri Fahrendorf's sentiments from a decade ago that even when she was an anomaly, when she got down to brewing talk, all demographic differences melted away. Customers: we can do better.

I have a personal theory that session beers (around five percent alcohol by volume [abv] or less) like those made by Benchmark became popular when brewers and beer reps started to turn from bearded young dudes into parents looking toward middle age. A couple nine percent double IPAs are harder to handle after forty or when you have little kids. This desire for a more traditional "European"-style beer (moderate alcohol, classic styles) has seen renewed interest as the industry moves into its fourth decade. Another sign of the industry's maturity is the built-in role of branding pros. Rachael supported this: "I would say that craft beer has grown up a lot in the last decade. Ten years ago, there were no marketers and there were no people in the office. There were no HR professionals. It really was just whoever was making the beer doing everything. I'm overgeneralizing, but that was much more common than it is now." Which was not to say that these are jobs better suited for women, but that the more organized, "businesslike," and possibly less insular workplace "creates a lot more space for diversity in general."

The craft beer movement not only brought fresher, better-tasting brews to North America, it brought a different kind of drinking space. The brewery taproom, like the biergartens of the Old World, represent a more relaxed, family-friendly setting in which to enjoy a moderate-abv beverage along with a little sunshine or the conversation of your community. Many tasting rooms around the country have different types of on-premise licenses, and unlike bars, they are often welcome to pets and children. It certainly has been a boon for the giant Jenga game industry. It was just this type of community space that appealed to L. A. McCrae, the brewmaster and voice behind Black Star Line Brewing, and inspired them to take on what would turn out to be a serious challenge.

Less than a month after the infamous 2017 white nationalist rally in Charlottesville, Virginia, *Vice* ran a story titled "This Craft Beer Forces

L.A. McCrae
Photo Courtesy of Black Star Line Brewing

You to Confront White Supremacy." The article profiled Black Star Line Brewing, then a fledgling start-up contract brewing in and around western North Carolina, "one of the first black, queer and female-owned and operated craft breweries in America." Without the grabby headline, the piece seemed an earnest take on some brewers trying to set up a space for people from all walks to get together and chill. This was not how the Trump-era public would receive it.

A few months later, an even more race-baiting headline appeared on *Vice*'s *Munchies* food vertical. This was an article by a different author that proclaimed "Owner of Queer, Black-Owned Brewery Says 'White Supremacy' Led to Its Closure."

As a good white liberal, I thought this was just such a shame. But there was nothing I could do about it from where I sat; the people in North Carolina sucked so much that they would prevent these oppressed-population brewers from running a peaceable business.

But of course, none of this captured the truth. In the meantime, a real brewery staffed by real people suffered the fallout.

L.A., a queer, masculine-of-center, gender-nonconforming woman who uses they/them/their pronouns, started out on a different path from most of the brewers I had spoken to. L.A.'s first calling was to ministry in the United Methodist Church. Following undergraduate study in political science and Africana studies, L.A. went to Wesley Theological Seminary in Washington, DC. There they focused on liberation theology, youth and young adult ministry, urban ministry, and community outreach.

However, at the United Methodist Church's General Conference in 2008, church hierarchy did not support LGBTQ clergy, upholding an earlier statement that homosexuality was "incompatible with Christian teaching." L.A. could not accept a vocation that would require them to be disingenuous about their feelings and identity.

Fast-forward a few years later, to 2014–15, and L.A. had since married, was living with their then wife in Knoxville, Tennessee. "I'd started my own insurance and financial services company and became a 'chamber fly.'" "Chamber" as in the chamber of commerce. As a small-business owner, L.A. "was going to all the chamber events and realized that a lot of these events took place at breweries. No one at these breweries, bars, restaurants, or taprooms looked like us," they noticed. "There were certainly no black women there, and there were no people of color."

L.A. started doing the math, thinking about how much money the chamber of commerce was dropping at these establishments.

"[My wife and I] realized that [the chamber of commerce was] extracting resources from underserved communities and often going to places...where folks that look like us just can't go. Even though they were in communities where we used to live. So we were looking at the intersections of gentrification, racism, classism, misogyny, patriarchy, all of this stuff in the rural South." I was humbly reminded of how easy it could be as a non-southern writer to comment about this and how this would be a great opportunity to just listen instead.

"I had a dream, since the age of fifteen, of creating a place called 'Home' that was a community space, a 24/7 coffee shop, that was there for the 'us-es' of the world." "Us," I imagined, meant those who would otherwise fear alienation, ostracism, or worse because of how they look and who they are.

"It became very clear to me that I was being called at that point to the [hospitality] industry." L.A. had found a love of craft beer through their older brothers. Growing up in Bel Air, Maryland, the McCrae siblings had bonded over the offerings of their local brewers. It seemed the perfect concept for their "place called home."

"I began to talk and brainstorm and set down some roots and see what might be possible. We settled down across the mountains over in Asheville [North Carolina] and were trying to be low-key" while the business came together. L.A. was a former community organizer and activist but had retired from this work, citing much of the heartbreak and burnout that plague activists. 2016 had other plans, though, and retirement became more and more difficult to maintain. "I got very involved in the Movement for Black Lives over in Asheville, and my partner at the time, Desaray, had

I had a dream, since the age of 15, of creating a place called 'Home,' that was a community space, a 24/7 coffeeshop, that was there for the 'us-es' of the world.

founded the local chapter of SURJ [Showing Up for Racial Justice]." There was a lot of "showing up" to do.

Candidate Trump came to Asheville, and L.A. and Desaray were arrested at a protest. Then the discriminatory HB2—North Carolina's so-called bathroom bill—passed, and L.A. was arrested again for protesting. As L.A.'s hospitality calling was becoming clear, their organizing work was becoming more challenging. "There was a lot of infighting in the Asheville organizing scene, and death threats. We were being threatened by white supremacists and actual police officers. So my partner and I and our son... had to leave Asheville...we were displaced for several months." They moved around the area, to Black Mountain, back to Asheville, and finally to Lake Lure, where they finally found the space to have a home-brew test lab. So they began test brewing while looking for a permanent commercial space and trying to lock in financing.

"After many, many, many countless hours of conversation with banks, CDFIs [community development financial institutions], all of them, we were just like, 'This dream's going to die. We cannot self-finance this.'" Nobody was lending. Then an opportunity arose: a recently closed brewery in Hendersonville, not far to the west, was for rent. The start-up costs would be slashed if they could move into a building already set up for brewing and didn't need to build it out.

L.A. had befriended brewery owners Joe Dinan and Lisa McDonald from Hendersonville's Sanctuary Brewing, a craft brewhouse with a social focus on animal welfare. Having them for neighbors seemed perfect, L.A. said: "I was learning from them; we have very similar missions, wanting to enact social justice with our beer." They were finally able to secure a small-business loan from an Asheville-based organization called Mountain BizWorks that focused on "entrepreneurs who have trouble securing funding from banks and other traditional sources," according to its website.

"Fast-forward again to 2017," L.A. told me, "and we were doing it for real. We started our first brews." Black Star Line Brewing put out its pilot batches. The brewery was named for Marcus Garvey's America-to-Africa transport line and featured pilot beers named for African American artists and activists such as the Stokely Stout and the Lorde Honey Pils—Lorde as in Audre. But things were not going to get easier.

"While we were doing all of that and [working] in the community and fund-raising, many members of my family became sick," their grandmother and oldest aunt included. "This was a really powerful moment, to have the matriarchs [fall ill] and to be the youngest granddaughter, sitting by my grandmother's deathbed."

While L.A. was sitting with their grandmother, they learned something eerily poignant: they were not the first brewer in the family.

"She said, 'I actually have a history of that good old home brew.' I was like, 'What? What are you talking about?' In her delirium she was telling me stories, and my aunt Georgie was telling me stories. They gave me recipes just off the top of their heads, and I learned that my uncles were involved and my grandfathers and cousins, so it was really fuel to my fire. I definitely felt I was at the intersection of social justice, ministry, and...my family calling. That's been really significant to me."

At that point, L.A. began to think of their brewing plans as more than a business: " It's close to home and feels like I'm responding to a calling."

Unfortunately, L.A.'s experience with Sanctuary Brewing in Hendersonville was not a faithful representation of the town as a whole.

"I did not do research on Hendersonville. I had no clue that seventy percent of people there voted for Donald Trump. I had no clue how racist and homophobic and sexist it could be." To add to that, "we were undercapitalized at loan origination from the lender, which was frustrating, but at this point it was a very interesting sequence of events."

I bet, I thought. Shortly after receiving a loan of about half their estimated start-up costs, the lender agreed to provide additional working capital, which, according to L.A., "never manifested." On top of the early funding problems, the brewery opened in November. "It was a really hard winter for a variety of reasons. The tourism was down. We knew going into it that we needed support during the winter."

While they were getting ready to open, supportive people from the community would come in with news from the neighbors. "They were like, 'Hey, this person doesn't want y'all to wear those black beer shirts'"—referring to the popular T-shirt that reads BLACK PEOPLE LOVE BEER. "'This person feels intimidated and threatened.'" Black Star Line and its taproom, Larry's Lounge (named after L.A.'s father, who liked to relax with a cold beer after a long day at work), was the only black, queer-owned nighttime venue in the area. LGBTQ locals would come in thanking them for opening the space. "We were the only gay/queer/black/people of color space in downtown Hendersonville, in all of Hendersonville to be frank. There are no gay places in this part of western North Carolina. There's no place for people of color to feel safe."

However, the grosser elements of Hendersonville took notice as well.

"We started to get hate messages on our social media, in our emails, on our phones—death threats—and the police weren't taking it seriously."

Frustrated by this, L.A. shared some of their experiences on their personal Facebook page. At first, the community rallied around them. "Once this stuff did go public, the community response was amazing. People came out and supported. Joe and Lisa over at Sanctuary hosted a day for us that was really awesome, other business owners came in and brought their teams, and the people of Hendersonville really did show up." Despite the unusually harsh winter, it seemed for a hot second that things might be okay. But even before the brewery opened to the public, the *Vice* story came out with its provocative headline.

The story went national and was picked up and shared around the web until even a writer in Los Angeles who was supposed to have her head buried in writing her own book heard about it. At first, seeing news about beer that "makes you confront white supremacy" felt like a good thing. We were all mad at white supremacists! Especially those of us who didn't have to deal with them on a daily basis! Of course, the revenue generated by my clicks went to the news sites, not the Black Star Line Brewery, and it was the latter that had to deal with the fallout.

"In hindsight, I wish I never would have shared that, because of course then people were saying we're doing this for a publicity stunt. We're just another minority-owned business crying racism. Mind you, people were breaking in. Our brewing system was vandalized. We had direct hate messages, death threats. People broke into our homes."

L.A. was discouraged. They retreated to the basement and focused on brewing. They felt that *Vice* had misrepresented their intentions—not to "force" confrontation but to start conversations about the culture and history represented by the brewery's offerings and mission.

"The first interview, we thought, was a really great interview, so we were shocked and surprised to see 'This Craft Beer Forces You to Confront White Supremacy.' That's the opposite of what we were doing. For me this really is about a ministry and creating space for whosoever.

"Because now, out of everything that happened, that *Vice* article has been the most damaging thing, because it got immediately picked up by all of these other news sources that didn't inspect the information, and people that I considered my best friends, family, community, completely abandoned me and the business." Friends felt alienated, were fearful of reprisals. Business was dismal. Owners of the only other black-owned business in town pulled L.A. aside, concerned about their safety. The Black Star Line team knew their landlord wanted them out, despite the fact that others in the building were further behind on rent because of the ruinous fiscal season they were all enduring.

The day after the brewery's Martin Luther King Day celebration, the team came to work to find the building locked. They had been evicted. Police were called. They were not allowed in to retrieve their personal items. *Munchies* published the second piece, detailing the brewery's closure, which is why I am not going to get into much detail about the reasons behind it here. I am less concerned with the nuts and bolts of the situation, of a business already struggling with stacked odds in the realms of financing and acceptance in a majority-hostile community, than with L.A.'s response. This was not, as it would probably have been for me, to curl up into the fetal position on my best friend's couch and never leave.

"So then the follow-up article, which was intentionally race-baiting, had an outdated picture of me holding a print of a quote that a black man said at our screening of *Selma*." The picture in question is one of L.A. in a hat and tank top, holding a screen-printed panel that reads I WANT BLACK BEER MADE BY BLACK PEOPLE,, with the bottom portion of the panel cut off. It is hard for me to see how this was so alienating for erstwhile friends. I'd love some beer made by black people, too.

"I wasn't saying Hendersonville is full of white supremacists. I was saying the institution of the landlord, the seller, and the CDFI conspiring, from the beginning, to underfund us...We have written proof that shows they were trying to get us out of the space. We were unlawfully evicted. But I can't call out white supremacy. There were other businesses in our building that were nine months behind on their rent. Ultimately what white supremacist institutions do is make the black, queer, person of color—whoever—business owner appear histrionic and unreasonable."

After the whole traumatic experience, L.A. took some time to recover. Not too long, though, as within a few weeks, the Black Star Line social media accounts were up and tweeting, speaking resilience and showing collaborations with other brewers. By the time I spoke to L.A., nearly four months later, they were already making plans to start contract brewing again. The dream of Black Star Line and the Larry's Lounge taproom was alive and kicking and looking for potential brewery sites in Washington, DC.

There is a whole lot more to say here about craft brewing being represented, since its beginnings in the 1980s, by hetero white dudes. Brewers of color such as L.A., Cajun Fire Brewing's Jon Renthrope, and beer influencers Teo Hunter and Beny Ashburn from Los Angeles's Dope and Dank are pushing forward the idea that craft beer can and does belong to them, just as Teri Fahrendorf asserted through experience and organizing that the brewhouse was a woman's place as much as anyone else's. The industry has a history of appealing to nonwhite non-dudes and also, tragically, of ignoring one of brewing's best talents: Annie Johnson.

"

I know that I've been
called to this moment and
that this brewery isn't just
about making great beer,
which we do; it's about
holding space for people
who need space. For people
who need community.

"

When Annie Johnson won the 2013 American Homebrewers Association Homebrewer of the Year award, she was the second woman and first African American to do so in its thirty-four-year history. The beer she won with was a light lager, difficult to brew and very difficult to win competitions with. Johnson had been brewing at home since 1999 and had won beer competitions in Germany and the United States, in addition to being a certified beer judge. According to an interview with Dave Infante from *Thrillist*, Johnson applied for brewing positions many times but never received responses. Which seems like the world's biggest shame, as most of us will never get to taste her beer.

The issue of exclusion in the beer community is an issue for both consumers and producers. It has to do with the ability to risk capital on business start-ups not known for huge profit margins, as well as changing perceptions of who exactly drinks craft beer. Creating spaces where women and people of color feel welcomed to come in and have a pint is crucial, which is just what the Black Star Line team is aiming for.

"I am a brewer, I come from a long line of brewers," L.A. told me. "This is the work that I'm being called to do. For quite some time I felt a lot of heaviness, because I wasn't able to follow my calling into the ordained pastoral ministry in the Methodist church, and I realize now that as much as things hurt, they all happen for a reason. Had I been able to be ordained, I would've never been here.

"I know that I've been called to this moment and that this brewery isn't just about making great beer, which we do; it's about holding space for people who need space. For people who need community. For people who are thirsty for more than just liquid, but really want that deep, intimate soul connection. I don't know how else it's going to work out, I don't know where this money is going to come from, but I'm going to keep pushing it."

Part Two:

Spirits With Roots

Makers and Boosters of Artisanal Liquor

As with beer, wine, and food, spirits consumers have become increasingly interested in the source of their libations in the past decade. Craft distilling faced an uphill battle in many US states and counties, where blue laws left over from the post-Prohibition moral panic exerted arcane restrictions on possible liquor makers. New York State and Colorado, notably, had active distillers' communities that successfully lobbied for policy changes in the late 2000s, kicking off craft spirits booms in both states. Be prepared for more: 2018 saw a significant reduction of the federal excise tax for small producers as a result of nationwide efforts by those in the craft spirits community. Now that one of the major obstacles to small producers on the federal level has been eased, who knows how many shiny new stills will start cooking. If the past five years have been any predictor, then many will be helmed by women.

. . . .

Mezcaleras and Madrinas

Just as whisky came back into fashion in the early 2000s after decades of being considered the province of old men with smoker's coughs, mezcal emerged from the villages of rural Mexico to become the toast of the global drinking elite in the 2010s. This occurred under various influences: foreign interest in Mexican cuisines, the industrialization and subsequent quality control problems in tequila production, a popular fervor for handcrafted and ancestral products, the cocktail renaissance, and, of course, the exquisiteness of the liquid itself.

I won't hide behind any pretense of objectivity when it comes to mezcal. Since my first exposure to a barely adequate brand in Brooklyn in 2011, I was intrigued. This was not the caustic, hallucination-inducing elixir I remembered Tom Cruise's character drowning his demons with in *Born on the Fourth of July*. It was, if not yet complex to me, intriguing. There was smoke and sweetness without the medicinal tang of peated Scotch, which I'd been trying to like for several years. After I moved to Southern California in 2014, it became an all-out obsession.

I was privileged with exposure to a cornucopia of mezcal brands while working under a bar director who (perhaps unwisely) had carte blanche with his liquor orders. The bar's bottom line's loss was our gain. I got to taste not only silky *espadín mezcales*, made from the most commonly cultivated agave species for mezcal, but took sips from rarer bottles marked with names in Spanish, Zapotec, and Nahuatl—*tobalá, tobaziche, dobadaán, tepeztate*. These tasted as different from one another as bourbon from gin.

I was late to this party, by industry standards. By 2014 mezcal had reached unprecedented popularity in the United States, Europe, and the urban centers of Mexico, where hip young Mexicans and plenty of tourists flocked nightly to *mezcalerías* that had sprung up within the past decade. Rural Mexicans had been making and drinking the stuff for centuries, with recipes and techniques that varied by region and from village to village. This was a true ancestral product, produced and consumed by farmers and their communities, often for special celebrations and religious occasions. It's a story that is easy to fall in love with, especially if you have a *copita* of 90-plus-proof liquor in your hand.

In brief: mezcal is a distilled spirit, protected under a *denominación de origen* (DOC) similar to those on Champagne, Napa Cabernet, and Comté cheese, which means it can be produced only under certain conditions. To be called mezcal, a spirit must be made in one of nine Mexican states designated in the DOC. It is made by fermenting the crushed, roasted hearts of maguey (agave) plants and running the resulting brew through a copper or clay still between one and three times. If you're wondering what the difference is between mezcal and tequila, let me preempt you: it's more than just the smoke. Mezcal enthusiasts remind us that tequila is just one of mezcal's offspring, a distilled spirit made from only one type of agave, cooked in masonry ovens or autoclaves rather than roasting pits. Tequila gained massive global popularity in the twentieth century, and its large-scale production dramatically affected the end product. Countless spirits enthusiasts bemoan tequila's "industrialization," as noted in the pointedly named *How the Gringos Stole Tequila* by Chantal Martineau. Greater efficiency means more profit for tequila companies and ostensible economic growth for the country, but the spirit's status has been widely downgraded to inexpensive booze for getting, as the kids say, shithoused.

Furthermore, as Martineau and others point out, the corporate-industrial business model more often than not leaves small farmers and farmworkers in peril, and the overcultivation of tequila's blue agave has led to a dangerous monoculture situation. It is a far cry from its ancestor mezcal's lovingly harvested, handcrafted reputation.

Smaller tequila brands have emerged since the rise of the premium market in the twenty-first century, harkening back to what old-school *mezcal de tequila* must have tasted like before consumer demand outpaced and outpriced traditional methods. These are wonderful, but there are dozens (some claim hundreds) of agave species used to make mezcal, which makes it an infinitely more fascinating subject for those of us who like to nerd out, hard.

The origin of mezcal's international boom is debated. Much credit is due to the Del Maguey brand and "Madrina" Misty Kalkofen, who spent years functioning as a volunteer brand ambassador in the United States until she officially got on the payroll in 2014 (see Misty's profile in chapter 9). While Misty was spreading the word to cocktail innovators in the United States, Yola Jimenez was in Mexico City, turning friends and travelers on to the spirit of Mexico by sheer force of fabulousness.

Gina Correll Aglietti is a stylish woman with a no-breaks conversational style, an erudite former New Yorker with fantastic glasses. I met up with her in Los Angeles one afternoon to discuss Yola Mezcal, a relatively new product on the LA bar scene at that time. Over lunch she told me the story of the fledgling company, which was mostly the story of Yola Jimenez, the brand's cofounder and a singular persona in the mezcal field.

Yola is the daughter of an academic and a lawyer, raised in Mexico City, educated in Europe, but with strong roots in Oaxaca. According to her friend Gina, Yola always had a special relationship with her grandfather, an engineer and avid mezcal collector who had returned from the capital to a village near his hometown in Oaxaca after retiring. He bought a farm in the heart of mezcal country, with a good water source and plenty of

Gina Correll Aglietti, Yola Jimenez, and Lykke Li
Photo Credit: Justin Tyler Close, provided courtesy of Yola Mezcal

wild agave growing around, and partnered with a *mezcalero* to make his own mezcal recipes. When her grandfather passed away, he left Yola the farm.

This was right at the beginning of mezcal's emergence into the global drinking consciousness, when many people in Mexico City still considered it a "peasant's drink," as Yola told Elise Taylor for *Vogue* in 2018. Rather than succumb to cultural pressures to leave again, Yola took over her grandfather's business and built a life around the liquid he loved.

Yola cofounded a tiny bar called La Clandestina with three partners in Mexico City. It was the first bar of its kind in the area, a space dedicated to a singular experience: "just mezcal, beer, and pepitas; some water," according to Gina. Bar shelves contained glass containers filled with whatever the proprietors had brought in from the countryside recently, with a good dose of mezcal education for the curious. It quickly became one of the highest regarded *mezcalerías* in the world.

As the owner of a respected bar and the friend of chefs, Yola became the person to know in Mexico City if you wanted to eat well. This is how she met Gina, introduced by a mutual friend when Gina was on a quest to find the "secret good stuff" in the Mexico City restaurant scene.

The two women clicked and spent much of the week of Gina's visit from New York together. In addition to getting the friends-and-family treatment at all those restaurants she'd been reading about, Gina had her first taste of mezcal, of which she said: "My mind was blown."

She returned to New York with a "suitcase full of mezcal," a familiar image from all the agave acolytes I've met. Gina was a chef at a speakeasy in Manhattan, and dismayed at how nearly impossible it was to obtain good mezcal. This was around 2009. The spirit's popularity was growing, but quality stuff was still not easy to find. All the while, every time someone she knew was headed to Mexico City, Gina sent them to Yola.

Years later, Gina was living in Los Angeles with her friend Lykke Li, for whom she had been working as a costume designer. Lykke is a Swedish musician who happened to provide the sound track to the mid-2000s for me. The two shared a house, work, and a social circle. On the second day of Lykke's own trip to Mexico City, a busy Gina wrote to tell her the name of her friend there. When Lykke received the message, she'd already been hanging out with Yola for two days.

When Yola visited her friends in Los Angeles and New York, she would bring glass jugs of her grandfather's recipes with her. The cool kids on America's coasts could not get enough, particularly of one recipe: a primarily *espadín* blend with "a touch of madrecuixe."

Gina recalled: "Everyone was calling us wanting mezcal. Everyone asked, 'When's Yola coming back?'"

At this same time Gina noticed something that annoyed her about the United States liquor market. In addition to a serious dearth of mezcal options, Gina said, "There [was] no alcohol targeted toward modern, smart women." "Women's" drinks all seemed to be lavender colored or focused on weightloss. Aside: Any sweet, technicolor bottled beverage with few to no calories is highly suspect and probably worse for you than sugar. Gina expressed her frustration, looking around the booze marketplace, at how few options there were for women interested in beautiful design and tasty, authentic drinks.

This brought me back to my experiences as a budding barfly in New York, guzzling what I presumed were "manly" beverages like cheap whiskey, not necessarily to emulate the men around me, but because so-called girlie drinks tended toward the saccharine—both in flavor and image. Even in my ill-spent youth, I knew this was someone else's construct of femininity, not to mention gross.

Yola's mezcal had a proven appeal across the gender spectrum. Gina, Yola, and Lykke decided to bottle and brand it in a way that appealed to their aesthetic sensibilities as well as their tastebuds. This was one reason to export. The other was Yola's vision of what her farm and production facilities could do within her community.

At university, Yola studied the benefits of economically empowering the women women in struggling communities. As reported in the World Bank's *World Development Report 2012*, when women control more household income, more resources go to the family than when men are

There [was] no alcohol targeted toward modern, smart women.

responsible for bringing wages home. With this in mind, Yola decided to employ all women on her bottling line and pay them directly. The more mezcal she sold, the more money she could invest back into the company, the more women she could hire. Gina explained: "Yola had been building up this farm to make it...sustainable, but she didn't necessarily want to make a big brand or bring it to America. We all started talking about it and realized it was something we wanted to do together. She had this amazing product, and she thought, 'I can make a direct impact on this community.'"

As of this writing, Yola Mezcal is available in dozens of on- and off-premise locations in New York and California.

While Yola Jimenez was enlightening artists in global cultural hubs, Bricia Lopez and Cecilia Rios Murrieta in Southern California were spreading the news about mezcal their own ways. Bricia does not own a liquor company, but she has possibly had the most mezcal cocktails named after her than anyone else. She is a lifelong ambassador of Oaxacan food and drink through her family's award-winning restaurant, Guelaguetza, in Los Angeles's Koreatown. The story goes: upon moving to LA from Oaxaca in 1994, her father, Fernando Lopez, discovered a large community of *oaxaqueños*, but none of the region's distinctive food. Some might have wallowed in homesickness; Lopez saw an opportunity. The original Guelaguetza opened in that same year, serving up southern Mexico's traditional moles and *tlayudas* with nary a crispy ground beef taco in sight. It was a truly daring move to start a "Mexican" restaurant in the '90s that deviated from the standard Americanized menu, but Lopez doubled down. If the Oaxacan community would eat there, others would notice. The following year his wife and children came to join him, bringing knapsacks full of cheese, tortillas, and mezcal from home. The small restaurant empire they built became a staple of Los Angeles dining, eventually earning a James Beard Award as an America's Classic.

Bricia Lopez
Photo Credit: Lily Ro Photography

In 2008 the financial crisis took its toll on the Lopez family businesses, and Fernando, Sr., sold off all his restaurants but one. Fearing the demise of their parents' legacy, Bricia and two of her siblings bought the Koreatown location from their parents, who then returned to Oaxaca. One of the next generation's first actions was to expand the space, including a sizable mezcal bar. Just as her father spotted an entrepreneurial niche to be filled back in 1994, so Bricia sensed that mezcal's time had come.

"I'd been living with mezcal basically since I was born," Bricia told me, in between the multiplicity of tasks involved in running a restaurant on a Thursday afternoon. Her father had made the spirit in Oaxaca prior to emigrating. Starting in 2000, Guelaguetza served what mezcal was available—about three brands, Bricia said. Around this time, Bricia began to notice more and more products marketed as "organic," "small batch," and "farm-to-table," which to her embodied what mezcal had always been. That, and the rise of classic cocktail bars in New York, San Francisco, and eventually Los Angeles, and she knew mezcal was "going to be huge."

Bricia wanted to use her platform as a restaurateur to help mezcal grow in the United States, to "speak on the category," and to educate consumers and encourage new brands. Bricia, with her brother Fernando, had become the public face of Guelaguetza and Oaxacan culture in Los Angeles, and mezcal was an intrinsic part of that. In 2013, Mayor Eric Garcetti pronounced Bricia the "official mezcalera" of Los Angeles. The role of ambassador and educator fit her well: she is outgoing and dazzlingly photogenic, her binational identity expressed through her personal style and passions. Here is a hip, young American urbanite telling you all about ancient culinary practices she learned firsthand from her grandparents. The bar community and food media fell hard for Bricia. Jonathan Gold called her a "Oaxacan Princess," and she and Fernando hosted nine episodes of *Eater*'s web series *Open Road*. She became the go-to authority on all things mole and mezcal for just about everyone, including the *New York Times*, the *New Yorker*, *Forbes*, and the Los Angeles Tourism Board, and she was included as one of "24 Restaurant-World Power Players Around the U.S." by Zagat.

She seemed the perfect immigrant success story, building a veritable brand empire by extolling her ancestral traditions. It had not always been so easy to feel at home, though. Like most immigrant children new to the United States, she struggled to feel accepted, particularly at a new school strictly divided along ethnic lines. Bricia found that even within the Mexican American community, Oaxacans faced prejudice—being, as she said, "a little shorter and a little darker." Oaxacan food and culture have only recently come to be regarded as important to the country's identity (at worst, trendy) in urban centers like Mexico City and Guadalajara, where even now bias exists against the predominantly indigenous people from more remote provinces. Before achieving popularity abroad, all the women mentioned in this chapter agreed: mezcal was considered the beverage of the poor, rural, and uneducated.

"Educating the Mexican community" about mezcal and her home state became a goal for Bricia, equally important as supporting the boom of new mezcal producers available north of the border and explaining the spirit to Americans.

For a few years in the early 2010s, cocktails with "Bricia" in the name could be found at many of LA's prime drinking dens, as the young restaurateur found kindred spirits in the budding cocktail scene. "There were only a few places in the beginning," she recalled. "Now, people just go to a restaurant and expect a great cocktail, but it wasn't like that before." As the scene grew, so did mezcal's popularity, to the point where Bricia felt like she had to step away. "It was almost too much," the volume of new brands coming in, and she could no longer be certain of ethical production and good compensation for growers in all cases. After pushing so hard for mezcal's acceptance, she found the category grown unwieldy, even unfamiliar.

Her new focus is telling people to go find out for themselves. "Go visit Oaxaca," she said, encouraging mezcal fans to journey to the source. The food and liquor are a gateway to the larger culture, one this *oaxaqueña* still tries to represent in all ventures. For now, Bricia and her siblings continue to focus on the restaurant, while she also engages in a variety of advocacy

I went to Oaxaca and I just fell in love. I loved everything about that place and I wanted a reason to be there. That's how I fell into mezcal.

for Latinx and Mexican American causes, and since becoming a parent, she records a podcast she hosts with her sister called *Super Mamás*.

Not far away in Orange County, Cecilia Ríos Murrieta was turning a passion for artisan agave spirits into an import/education/advocacy business as "La Niña del Mezcal" (the mezcal girl). Another truly bicultural entrepreneur, Cecilia has been volleying back and forth between Mexico City and California since she was five years old. The child of a tight-knit, entrepreneurial family, Cecilia's parents followed work opportunities from Cuernavaca to Anaheim and back throughout her life. As a college student in Mexico City studying business administration and working part-time as a researcher at an NGO, Cecilia's career would ostensibly follow a steady nine-to-five track headed straight to an air-conditioned office. That was, until she took a trip south with some friends.

"I went to Oaxaca and I just kind of fell in love. I loved everything about that place and I wanted a reason to be there. That's how I fell into mezcal." This is a common theme among mezcal lovers, of being so enchanted by the culture and food that they want to bottle the experience, or at least part of it. It happened to Del Maguey's Ron Cooper, to Pierde Almas founder Jonathan Barbieri, and definitely to Cecilia, who became the woman around town who wanted you to try mezcal. The name "La Niña del Mezcal" was born out of how friends started referring to her. By 2011, she turned her passion for the spirit into a social media presence and blog. Followers of the blog were soon contacting her to ask where they could find the fantastic bottles she wrote about, and from there came the next step—Cecilia would head back to the country to start her own mezcal brand by partnering with producers whose mezcal she loved.

There was just one hang-up: "Once I told my mom that I was going to go to Oaxaca to make mezcal...she's a little protective. The idea of her daughter running off into the Oaxacan sierra, going into this world of men, was not her ideal situation for me. So she said, 'If you're going to do it, I'm just going to go with you.'"

Working as a team, the *mujeres* Murrietas made their first deal with a *mezcalero* a few months later—a handshake agreement with a distiller who would provide them with liquid and nothing else. That left bottling, labeling, licensing, marketing, distribution, and so much more for them to figure out. As Cecilia told me on the phone from Mexico City, "Once we had the juice, basically, we had to set up an entire business. And that was my job." She took her policy research experience and went to work. "I kind of researched my way into becoming a legitimate business, exporting mezcal by myself and going through all of the processes of trademark registration. I did it all by myself. Everyone said, 'Hire a lawyer for this,' and I was like, 'Nah!'"

Through lots of online digging and applications, not to mention a few hard sells from Cecilia's indefatigable mother, the two-person operation produced its flagship mezcal. Their handshake agreement with their supplier took place in March. By October, La Niña del Mezcal Espadín was in the warehouse, ready to go.

The first time I tried a La Niña del Mezcal offering, I had no idea this was a two-women show. All I knew, as I scanned the bottles at LA's Tintorera bar, was that La Niña made a sotol. Sotol is another Mexican spirit made from a plant called the desert spoon, or *Dasylirion wheeleri* if you want to get technical. The spoon is not an agave; it is supposedly a close relative of asparagus. I have no idea how that works. I do know I was curious enough to drop something like twenty dollars on a single glass of the stuff, because that is what we do. "We" meaning those of us sufficiently obsessed with artisanal spirits that we can't resist trying every damn thing on the shelf. We are La Niña's bread and butter—those who would follow her blog, with its photos of mountain landscapes with voluminous cloud towers overhead and rows of spiny agaves, and drink our mezcal, dreaming of the decade of Mexican sunshine that went into that glass. I am well aware that this idea of a sacred, ancient product made by rugged farmers in remote villages is embedded in the marketing, and it's clearly not the whole story, but I was happy to be a bit of a sucker at that moment. The sotol was worth it—funky on the nose and soft on the palate, with lingering notes of cinnamon. I'd take one of those over three cheap margaritas every day of the week.

I researched my way into becoming a legitimate business, exporting mezcal by myself and going through all of the processes of trademark registration. I did it all by myself. Everyone said 'hire a lawyer for this,' and I was like 'nah!'

A few months after my conversation with Cecilia, she left La Niña del Mezcal, the young entrepreneur ready for the next challenge. Her new venture, ŌME Spirits, incorporates one type of agave from two far-apart regions of Mexico as an exploration of terroir.

As with so many local products that have roused international demand, there are risks to the fast-rising popularity of mezcal. Tequila blew up in global markets in the twentieth century, and those who study these spirits bemoan how profit-driven production methods have led to the current status of mass-market tequila as a rotgut shooting spirit. How agave spirits are produced and the impact on the communities that make them have been the focus of a growing number of books over the past five years. Of the twenty-two volumes that turn up on a search for books on mezcal and tequila, fifteen were written by women. These volumes—notably by sociologists Sarah Bowen and Marie Sarita Gaytán, agronomist Ana G. Valenzuela-Zapata, and journalists Chantal Martineau and Emma Janzen—delve into the ethical puzzle of agribusiness, while somehow managing to reinforce the magical draw of these spirits. Why are so many women writing about mezcal? For one, it is delicious. But it's a growing social concern, with the tequila industry's weakening agave monoculture and the fate of Jalisco's small farmers serving as a cautionary tale. There is danger involved when an artisanal product becomes popular overseas. Much like Peruvian farmers who one day discovered they could no longer afford to eat the quinoa they grew, there is fear that mezcal's high price abroad will take it away from those for whom it was once part of daily life. Additionally, agave is a slow-growing plant, taking between seven and thirty-five years to mature. Overharvesting of the agave plants could be catastrophic, but demand keeps rising. Valenzuela-Zapata and Gaytán, like Bricia Lopez and Cecilia Murrieta, strive to educate the world on these beverages as part of their heritage that is important and worth saving.

In her book *Divided Spirits*, Bowen recounts years spent talking to agave farmers, *mezcaleros*, spirits company executives, brand entrepreneurs, and CRT representatives. Her studies took her on long solo trips through the Jaliscan and Oaxacan countryside and into the depths of federal bureaucracy to talk to someone on every level of the debate. She extended her interviews to American hipster bartenders, whom she characterized with as much empathy and skepticism as an academic Joan Didion. Bowen committed an entire appendix in her book to detailing how her gender affected her interactions with the by far majority men she observed and interviewed in the writing. This includes how she deflected dinner invitations from interview subjects and how she approached rural *mezcaleros* who just did not know what to make of this random American woman coming around and asking about their distillation methods. Interestingly enough, she commented that in some cases, sexism helped her research, as male executives revealed sensitive or ethically questionable information, figuring it would all be over her head.

Of the brand boosters and bottlers, though, the hopeful refrain was one I've heard from women across all alcohol fields: once you start talking shop, people care less about your gender. The existing boys' club of liquor distributors aside, those with real skills tend to give credit where it is due. Bartenders can be convinced to carry a brand with a single taste, so Gina and Yola went straight to them and sold directly to bars and retail stores. Likewise Cecilia Rios Murrieta, having done all the work to create a brand on her own, was not about to be cowed by meetings with suits. Cecilia knew, she told me, that what she made was great, and anyone she'd want to do business with would taste that.

Rum Runners

I was not expecting a discussion of terroir when I called up Karen Hoskin in Crested Butte, Colorado, to talk about her company, Montanya Distillers. First, the company name is pronounced the same way as *montaña*, the Spanish word for "mountain," for reasons that will soon become obvious. Rum is made from cane sugar and its by-products, hardly an agricultural mainstay of the Rocky Mountains, and the idea of a Rocky Mountain rum's flavor being rooted in a sense of place was incongruous. Her story, though, spoke of a passion brought home and made local.

I'd tasted Montanya Oro at my aforementioned easygoing bar in Los Angeles. I'd recommend it when customers asked for rums we didn't have, like Mount Gay or Bacardi Gold, as it was a solid amber rum that mixed well. I did not know who was behind this label and all the other reasons to be drinking it, until another interviewee told me I had to talk to Karen. Calling her up, I was curious about even the obvious. Why rum? Why Colorado?

"It goes back I guess almost ten years now," Karen began, then paused. "Of course, it goes back a lot further than that. I've been a rum fanatic ever since I was probably nineteen years old, when I discovered rum was one of the only spirits I could drink without feeling terrible the next day."

Karen Hoskin
Photo Courtesy of Montanya Distillers

I have heard this from spirits lovers about every category. From the agave evangelists who swear mezcal is hangover-free to the gin-thusiasts who will tell you that certain botanicals are anti-inflammatory, people gravitate toward the alcohol source that makes them feel the least terrible. As drinking strong liquor of any sort is a taste one acquires over time, this makes a lot of sense, though I have yet to find any real science behind the assertions. For everyone who swears bourbon or tequila or vodka has never let them down, there is a matching population who will never touch the stuff again. But as my physician father used to tell us: even if it's psychosomatic, it's still working.

Karen's magic liquor was rum, and she became a hobbyist, trying different varieties, visiting distilleries, making cocktails and her own infusions. She called it a "little love affair for a very long time." Her professional life took a more practical turn. Karen has a master's degree in public health and worked in public health for many years. She also had experience in nonprofit administration, graphic and web design, and marketing before rum even came into the picture. She was working as a freelance brand expert for other people's companies when she had one of many aha moments, as she called them. "About ten years ago...I quite literally woke up one morning and said to my husband, 'Hey, I have to make a change. I've spent all this time doing these projects and I gave everything away at the end of the day to help build these other companies."

She had had several careers, a good marriage, and two children, but she wanted something tangible to take away from "all the energy [she'd] been putting out into the universe." What happened next may have had something to do with the fact that they were on an island in Belize while traveling through Central America.

"We'd been not only drinking rum cocktails, but we'd just gone to Guatemala. I was inspired by a couple of different things on that trip. One was that there's a whole mountain tradition of rum making which I did not know that much about until then. Also, there was this incredibly strong tradition of women making interesting things, producing cool products. Ron Zacapa in Guatemala, which is an amazing rum distillery, had a female lead in their distilling operation. That was really eye-opening for me because she was the first female in the industry that I'd ever come across."

The "female lead" Karen referred to was master blender Lorena Vásquez of Zacapa rum, which in recent years has played a significant role in the effort to lift the category's reputation up from cheap mixing liquor to sippable spirit. After moving from her native Nicaragua to her then husband's home in Guatemala during the Nicaraguan war, Vásquez found work in a brewery. She had studied pharmaceutical chemistry, though, and beer didn't do it for her. Rum turned out to be her medicine of choice. After leaving the brewery and her marriage, she found her place in the Zacapa quality control department, ascending to the top job over almost three decades. She credits her (legendary) sense of smell for her success as a blender, though one suspects her reputedly merciless attention to detail helped as well. It was Vásquez who began aging the rum—made from fresh cane juice instead of molasses—at a facility 2,300 meters (about 7,550 feet) above sea level, for what Zacapa's literature calls "slow maturation," out of the subtropical valley heat. According to Montanya, a high-altitude microclimate has a greater daily range in temperature, allowing for an expansion and contraction of the barrels that actually hastens the aging process. Either way, Guatemala's specific geography is key to Zacapa's velvety, complex final incarnation, and attachment to its place is important to the brand. To add to the local loyalty, Vásquez frequently touts her commitment to employing indigenous women in crafting the petate, or woven palm fiber, rings that encircle the twenty-three-year-old and *reserva* bottles.

"Coming across Ron Zacapa was a real eye-opening moment," Karen Hoskin told me. Through her rum tasting, education, and distillery visits, she'd encountered an industry that was "totally male-dominated." That there was a woman in charge of a rum distillery way up in the Guatemalan highlands struck a chord.

"I'd come across women having interesting businesses and heading up interesting projects, but not very many products. That was the aha moment,

Ron Zacapa in Guatemala, which is an amazing rum distillery, had a female lead in their distilling operation. That was really eye-opening for me because she was the first female in the industry that I'd ever come across.

back in 2008. There was this whole convergence of different things at a particular moment in time that caught me, and I just said, 'I could do this.' There was a whole tradition of mountain rum that I could emulate in some ways."

Karen "jumped ship on [her] business and decided to go a different direction." She wasted no time. Four months later, "I had a TTB license, a still, and all my compliance to be able to make rum and have a tasting room and do everything legally. That was where it all started."

This quick start-up surprised me. I had heard plenty of horror stories from would-be distillers about archaic state and local regulations, hapless inspectors, and killer excise tax rates. Husband-and-wife team Melkon Khosrovian and Litty Mathew of Greenbar Distillery, for example, jumped through countless hoops to become the first distillery in the city of Los Angeles since Prohibition—in 2012. County regulations on distilling facilities had not been reassessed in decades. Being pioneers brought significant challenges and not insignificant expense—manageable only because Greenbar had sizable success with its original facility in nearby Monrovia and had the support of a local lawmaker. In the six years since Greenbar's opening, sweeping changes have been made through state legislation, and four new distilleries have sprung up in LA County. I had to know how Karen had seemingly glided through this process.

Karen elaborated: it was by no means easy, but a few key things worked in her and her husband Brice's favor. For one, they were used to paperwork. "It was a lot of compliance. We...had to jump through a lot of hoops, but I was quite accustomed to that, and my husband was quite accustomed to that, so it wasn't very hard for us. I think a lot of people who get into the craft spirits industry do it because they're creative types and they want to make something, and I don't think the personality type is always compatible with having to do excise taxes twice a month and having to submit all the reports that we submit. There's a huge administrative side to owning a craft distillery that a lot of people probably wouldn't do well with. But because I came more from the business side, rather than the creative/making things side, it just wasn't overwhelming to me at all."

Their location was helpful as well: "The state of Colorado is very gentle to distilleries. We have great laws here, we always have, I think, because of the beer and wine industries here that led the way." Coloradans were no strangers to the economic benefits of local booze. "I never really understood how great it was going to be, doing this in Colorado, until I was already in the business, and I started traveling and realizing how many benefits we had in Colorado that other states could not offer." Her tasting room, for example was an important source of exposure and revenue: "There were very lean years, early on, when I was surviving because I had a tasting room, not because I had a wholesale business. As a result, I was able to bankroll some things with the tasting room that other states, they just didn't offer that. You couldn't have a tasting room and sell cocktails and really have a full bar setting, so I'm lucky."

Karen grew up in Maine and met her husband at college in Massachusetts. After a decade living in Arizona, Brice doing environmental consulting and Karen working in politics and nonprofits, the two returned to Brice's home state of Colorado. They kept busy. During their twenty-seven-year marriage, Karen speculated they've started six businesses between them. This is impressive, but the alcohol business is its own animal.

"I'm really aware of how little I knew about the industry going in. I literally had no understanding of how spirits were sold, how spirits were distributed...If I had it to do over again, I would have spent the first three months deeply studying the industry. I just assumed that it was like groceries or anything else. I had no idea of how complicated and how mafia-ish it can be."

According to Karen, the liquor industry involves some "very long-established families and very long-established ways of doing business that flow out of Prohibition." Other companies, she said, hire their first employee straight from the somewhat monolithic distribution industry, someone who "comes in as an informant and says, 'Well, if you want to do that, you're going to have to do this.'" Montanya did not have that, which she speculated probably contributed to their particular character.

I'm really aware of how little I knew about the industry going in. I had no understanding of how spirits were sold, how spirits were distributed... If I had it to do over again, I would have spent the first three months deeply studying the industry.

"We didn't do anything the normal way," she said with a chuckle. "That made us feel very authentic and interesting and different, I think... but it also meant that it has taken longer and has taken more, probably— more hours and more energy. It was a bit like going to grad school at the same time as running a business." Trial by fire, she called it. "It's not unlike me to do something I've never done before, but it's really unlike me to not spend a long time reading and educating myself about something in advance or early in the process."

Wasn't that the thing, though, I wondered, that spurred her forward with this huge change? That sense of *I have to do this NOW*.

"I just jumped into it totally. I kept my day job for about a year, but, wow, I had no idea what I was taking on. It's just so many little things. I didn't have a business plan, I didn't think a lot of things through."

Despite this learning curve, she did have a few legs up on the process. When I asked if anything from her prior businesses was useful in her rum venture, she was emphatic.

"Oh gosh, yes. Everything," she said, laughing. "I ran [a public health] clinic in northern Arizona for about six years, and I had about thirty employees over that time. I learned a lot about managing people in my nonprofit days. I built a preschool and I worked for an organization that did a lot of crisis-intervention-type stuff straight out of college. Just from the very early times, I worked with large groups of people and that really helped me to understand a lot of the interpersonal aspects of being an employer." Montanya currently employs twenty-three people at the distillery and tasting room in Crested Butte. "It's a constant process of just making sure that we're being great employers. I don't think I could have come into that cold and done as well as I have if I hadn't had all that previous experience."

With this combination of geography, work ethic, and business acumen, the company stuck. Now in its tenth year, the rum is available in forty-two states and seven countries outside the United States. Karen and Brice are vocal advocates of sustainability, running the distillery on 100 percent wind power and taking a long, long list of actions to lessen the business's impact on the environment. Their sugarcane is sourced from Louisiana, the glass bottles are American made, and they have an outspoken commitment to paying employees above industry norms. Their mission is to become a zero-waste facility.

Karen was forty-one years old when Montanya was born, and her two sons were seven and nine. I asked how running a distillery affected her family—a question I am always a little hesitant to ask, since women, more than anyone, bear the brunt of social scorn for any perceived parenting infractions. She had broached the topic earlier, though, and I was curious to see how distillery children panned out.

"My kids have grown up in the facility and in a bar, which is kind of funny. But they're total entrepreneurs and hard workers. They know how to bottle rum and they know how to make rum and they give amazing tours. It's pretty fun to have them now, as one of them is nineteen and one of them is seventeen. It's really a family business in every way." There is a certain amount of stigma, though, isn't there? Did she ever worry about how the constant presence of hard alcohol might affect her kids? Did anyone throw shade at them?

"I feel like it's been amazing for my kids on so many levels. I'm a big fan of just modeling to my kids rather than trying to be instructive. For them to see us having an alcohol company but also having extremely responsible decision-making choices around alcohol, period, has been inspiring. Both of my kids, as teenagers, have been really responsible with alcohol, which not everybody is when they're seventeen and eighteen. Also, for my boys, growing up in a house with a female business owner, I think it has been interesting for them on a lot of levels because, first of all, they see how much I struggle some days."

Karen's family and friends act as her allies when she encounters sexism on the job, rather than her having to voice any frustrations aloud. She seems thankful for this and also feels it gives those close to her an important perspective—particularly her sons.

"How [my work] is and has been—filled with a lot of sexism—if anybody sees that and experiences it alongside me, it's my husband and my kids and my best friends. It's not my coworkers; it's not my employees. [My family has] had an opportunity not only to think about equal rights from a more philosophical perspective, but to actually see when it is in action—and when it's not in action. They've been there for me through a lot of rough moments and I really appreciate it."

Here is another point I'm happy she brought up, since I am sometimes reticent to dive in for the "What discrimination or harassment have you encountered?" conversation. It's a huge issue, but many women bristle at this line of questioning, preferring to focus on their accomplishments rather than horrible people they'd met along the way. I understand this, not wanting to give any airtime to those who perpetuate bad behavior or, at the very least, to appear to revel in one's own potential disenfranchisement. On the other hand, social currents in the past few years have been based on the principle that sharing the stories of one's own hardships helps others who might be experiencing the same. Karen was forthcoming, and though I am not a business owner (*yet*), her candor was edifying.

"[There are] so, so many stories I could tell you." She laughs and sighs a little. "I guess probably the one that struck [my family] the most was, recently, I went to make a presentation about the company, so I dressed up a little bit. I was in a white lace shirt and had a box in my arms of printed decks—informational decks about the company. I walked into a room of angel-type investors, very, very established businessmen. They were all sixty and over and all white. They thought I was there to deliver their lunch. For the first ten minutes, they treated me like I was the lunch person."

"Oh my god," I said, "really?"

Sure enough: "It took me a while to figure out why they were talking to me so strangely and why they were asking me what I brought them, what we were having, clearing things off for me to set up on the side of their meeting room. I was like, *What's going on here?* Then it finally dawned on me and I said, 'Actually, I'm your next presenter.' They all straightened up and were like, 'Sorry, we thought you brought our lunch.' It was just a moment of like, wow, we have not actually come very far."

Even among her own board members, Karen said, old attitudes can surface unexpectedly.

"Another moment was when I was meeting with one of my investors. He's also over sixty, a white guy. I was, for the first time, expressing to him that I might like to consider hiring a CEO. I've been the CEO for almost ten years and I feel in many ways like someone else could maybe do a better job. I have a bit of founder's syndrome. I was talking with him and he started describing [a new CEO], he just said, 'If you hire a CEO, he's going to want a piece of the company and he's going to want this kind of salary, and he's going to want this and that.'

"He literally went on for fifteen minutes describing my replacement, and the whole time I was just like—my heart physically hurt. I was like, 'Basically, what you're saying is my replacement needs to be a man, first of all. Second of all, he's going to want all these things and they're things that I don't get right now?' This is my company, I built it and I don't get paid that salary. I've created several-digit growth every year—24 percent growth, 30 percent growth. So it's not like I'm failing—this is my place. It was funny because my toes were curling up in my shoes; I was having this intense physical reaction.

"Finally, I just stopped and then I said, 'Bill, I really want to listen to you right now, but your gender pronouns are all male and it's offending me.' I just said, 'It's very possible that we might hire a female CEO for Montanya. Who knows? I think we should be objective and I think we should keep our minds open.'

"He was very constrained and he said, 'I'm just an old guy . . .'" She laughed again, remembering the discomfort. "It's just stuff like that—being at the bar after a meeting with distributors or sales reps and really having to say, 'This is not appropriate behavior with me.' I'm their business associate, I'm not there to be a sexual object at eleven o'clock at night."

It's constant, she said. She gets tired of it, of course. Unexpected revelations do occur, though, and when they do, it's wonderful. Her son is a business student, and a few weeks earlier, he had come along to watch a presentation she gave to her company. His reaction was more mature than

...being at the bar after a meeting with distributors or sales reps and really having to say, 'This is not appropriate behavior with me.' I'm their business associate, I'm not there to be a sexual object at eleven o'clock at night.

one might expect from a nineteen-year-old: "Mom, I know you've known these people for [years], but they're impressed by you." Her employees were fans, and it reinforced that she had been doing things the right way.

For me, it was heartening to hear a woman honestly acknowledge strength and accomplishment without a veil of self-deprecation.

"I've also made huge progress...to give female business owners in the distillery business a good reputation, and set a good example."

Much like agave liquors, rum has gained a new global respectability through the cocktail renaissance. It's been a misconception among drinkers at northern latitudes for decades that liquor made from sugarcane is suited only to highballs or drinks that come with baroque straws. Helped by the *new* new tiki drink revival (personally, I think tiki never went anywhere, it just adapted), the mystifying intoxicant known as "kill devil" has become an intellectual pursuit.

One rallying cry of rum geeks (rum-inators? rum-pires?) is the lack of firm international regulations on what the name actually means. It is difficult to establish a notion of a product having a sense of place when it lacks an official homeland. The category has no denomination or appellation to guarantee quality, no international trade agreements to protect its reputation around the world. In the United States, it must be made from sugarcane, which can take the form of refined or unrefined sugar, cane juice, or molasses (molasses is the natural by-product of sugar refinement). Even this has seen some wiggle room, as with certain American "rums" made from sugar beets.

While the Caribbean certainly claims the most distinguished rum-making and -drinking traditions in the world, even among the island distillers there are widely varying ideas of what "true rum" is. English-speaking islands' rum is different from Spanish-speaking islands' *ron*, which both vary from French-speaking islands' *rhum*, not even touching on newly exported artisan cane spirits such as *aguardientes de caña* and *clairin*, coming out of Mexico and Haiti, respectively.

Differing tradition is one thing, but a major point of contention is the addition of sugar. Some distillers in Guatemala and Venezuela, for instance, say that adding sugar or other flavoring elements after distillation is a part of their tradition, while adding sugar to finished rum is forbidden in Jamaica and Martinique. As its popularity grows, rum's crusaders are calling for greater clarity in labeling.

If anyone can make my orthodoxy-averse brain embrace a crusade for purity, it's Joy Spence. The woman is a legend, an innovator, a boss. Since 1997, she has served as master blender of Appleton Estate; by all known accounts, she was the first woman in the world to achieve the title.

As noted in Fred Minnick's *Rum Curious*, the history of rum in the Caribbean is a story of slavery, colonialism, sugar plantations, and pirates. The rum industry's growth in former English colonies such as Jamaica and Barbados was spurred substantially by the British naval tradition of rum rations for sailors, who received a daily booze allotment from the Crown from 1731 up until the 1970s. Rum was sailors' drink of choice, and where the navy docked, rum makers prospered.

Appleton Estate in Jamaica's Nassau Valley has been growing and distilling sugarcane since 1749. Appleton's signature blends have been go-tos for craft bartenders over the past decade, as they are reasonably priced, quality aged rums with a distinct Jamaican flavor. These were the workhorse rums at my first craft bar job, when the retro new wave Smith and Cross was too hot (or too pricey) for your average mai tai. Appleton twelve-year-old is dark amber, with a slight hogo tang and a splash of orange zest. It is one of five year-round offerings from the company, which include a fifty-year bottling. Because of Jamaica's labeling standards, this means all rums in the blend are at minimum fifty years old; some may well be older.

According to the distillery, it adds no additional sugar or flavorings to its rum; the rum's dark, sweet, mild funk comes only from fermentation, distillation, and barrels. And, of course, hitting the right balance in the blend.

This is where the master blender comes in. She is responsible for the chemical and sensory makeup of the final product, and the outcome of every bottling depends on her nose. It's a big deal. The first time I met Joy Spence, she was receiving the Pioneer Award from Tales of the Cocktail's Dame Hall of Fame in New Orleans. I was awed to shyness. My boyfriend, a photographer, suggested I say hello. I had been telling him all week how Spence's honoree status was a principle reason I'd bought the tickets to the ceremony, which, to a writer riding on her last available credit card balance, was no small thing. I finally coyly asked for a photo. I live in Los Angeles and have made drinks for Oscar winners and teen idols and not batted a single eyelash. But this was different. She was just so cool.

I needn't have worried. Joy is gracious and down-to-earth and extremely active in the global spirits community. She is clearly inspired by her work and open to questions. She was introduced at the ceremony by Ian Burrell, the UK-based global ambassador for the entire rum category. Burrell talked about the reasons he refers to Joy as "Aunty," not only because of their close professional relationship but because of the knowledge she laid on him throughout the years. Burrell related a story about when he was first looking to work with Appleton in the UK. Joy came to do a training for him and other bartenders. She took them through an exercise, to make their own blended rum by mixing from bottles in the bar. She would then smell it, analyze it, and pick the best blend from the bunch. As a "brash little young upstart in the industry," he wanted to "pull one over on a master blender," whom he thought were all "overpaid, overrated." So he just got his favorite rum and submitted that as his sample.

Joy assessed the thirty-some-odd "blends," which were each labeled with its creator's initials. She picked his up and asked, "I.B.? Who is I.B.?"

"I was like, *Yes! I've won the competition!*" Burrell remembered with a chuckle. He said that after smelling his "creation," she looked at him and said, "This is just Appleton twelve-year-old." Busted!

Burrell said he then realized what a master blender is all about. "It's not just about picking out rums from different barrels; it's about

Hope Ewing and Joy Spence
Photo Credit: Tuan Lee

We're bartenders, we're bar owners, we're ambassadors, we're decision makers, we're trendsetters, we're mentors, and most importantly, we are friends. We are united in making this industry an inclusive space for all.

understanding what goes behind the rum. The heart and soul of the product." He called the spirits industry an old boys' club, particularly in the "blending game," in which the title of master blender is passed from father to son in many companies. Despite her humility, "this lady pioneered her way in this industry."

Joy took the podium to booming applause, dressed in a lively patterned dress, wearing bright red lipstick, and standing with a bearing that told us she was, indeed, the (benevolent) boss.

She thanked Burrell and the Dame Hall of Fame, saying, "My gratitude, like my rum collection, is very large."

She told the crowd that when she was appointed back in 1997, she didn't think very much of the fact that she was the first woman in the world to have the position at a major distillery. She was just a person doing the job that she loved. Twenty years on, women like "Lorena from Zacapa, Marianne [Barnes] from Castle and Key, or Rachel [Barrie] from Morrison Bowmore" are in top positions at major brands. "In Jamaica, we say 'big up to these ladies.'" She reiterated the importance of women in the spirits industry, and "not just at distilleries. We're bartenders, we're bar owners, we're ambassadors, we're decision makers, we're trendsetters, we're mentors, and, most importantly, we are friends. We are united in making this industry an inclusive space for all, no matter our gender, color, heritage, sexual orientation, or religion. I feel immensely fortunate that my thirty-five-year tenure at Appleton has allowed me to pursue my passions. Passion is what it takes to make a mark in this world."

Her philosophy of making a living through what one is passionate about was clear in everything she said. During the Q&A section of the Dame Hall of Fame event, in response to a question about advice the honorees would give to their fifteen-year-old selves, Joy brought up her experience giving motivational talks to high school students.

"I tell them to think outside the box. Do not follow your parents. Follow what you have a passion for—that is how you are going to be successful, following your dream. I have been able to convert a lot of doctors into distillers," to the chagrin of many mothers, she added. This conviction was born of personal experience: she went on to recall how as a university student, her and her contemporaries' lives were very much dictated by their parents. She said that her two grown children have always been encouraged to choose their own paths.

"Many of my classmates, when they got their various degrees, they handed the paper to their parents and said, 'Here, take it. Now I'm going to do what I want to do.'"

Joy became interested in chemistry at thirteen, the story goes, due to the encouragement of a favorite teacher. She had not been doing well in class, and her instructor took special interest in Joy, so much so that she wound up earning the highest mark in the class. Tragically, this beloved instructor died the following year. The teenage Joy was devastated and vowed to honor her mentor by becoming "the best chemist there is." She followed through. Everywhere she went, she came in first in her class. After high school she headed to the University of the West Indies, then to Loughborough University in England for a master of science in analytical chemistry, achieving the top exam score there as well. Throughout her career, Joy has been awarded numerous honors, including the Order of Distinction from the Jamaican government in 2005 and honorary doctorates from Loughborough University and the University of the West Indies. But as with most people in the spirits industry who didn't inherit their jobs, she came by her career somewhat circuitously. When I called her at home in Jamaica, I wanted to know what her original plan out of school had been.

"Actually I wanted to do medicine, but when I went to university I realized I just couldn't handle trauma. I would just freeze, so I wouldn't be a help to anyone. I decided to go and lecture in chemistry," but she got restless teaching. Joy is a person of vast energy who loves dancing. And working with heavy industrial equipment, apparently. "After a while, I wanted to get some actual manufacturing experience, so I joined Tia Maria [liqueur] as a research chemist. After two years as a research chemist I joined Appleton as a chief chemist. That's when I got into distilling."

After joining Appleton in 1981, Joy began working closely with Master Blender Owen Tulloch, who clearly saw something in her, and added to her skills as a scientist. At this time, Joy said she "became totally fascinated with what they call the sensory art of rum making and how complex a spirit it is. I started to enjoy the beautiful complex flavors and aromas that are present in rum. I tutored with [Tulloch] for a few years, and then when he retired in 1997 that's when I was appointed master blender."

She did not know it at the time, but in 1997 there was no other woman in the world with this title. The master blender, like a master distiller, oversees all aspects of the production of her spirit. In addition to having authority over the fermentation and distilling processes, it is ultimately the MB's job to "make" the spirit. The idea of spirits blending has gotten some shade thrown at it in the past decade, due to the rise of single-estate tequila and single-barrel bourbons and the negative associations with cheap blended whisky. But even the fanciest single malt requires the touch of a blender to make each bottle the best it can be (note: "single malt" means a whisky is made from 100 percent malted barley at a single distillery, not that it all comes from the same barrel). Barrels vary in the flavors they impart over time, and whether its cognac, rum, whisky, or anything else, the responsibility of the blender is to select the right quantity of spirit from each cask for the flavors she wants to express. It is, as Joy noted, a complex sensory art.

I asked if she faced any resistance within the company upon her promotion to the top job. She responded that no one was surprised, as she had been working closely with Tulloch for years. Her colleagues "knew that would just be a natural upward movement for me." It is worth noting here that the two master rum blenders mentioned, like Anne-Françoise Pypaert of Brasserie d'Orval, rose to their positions after decades with the same company. Even in very old-school environments, loyalty and proven expertise triumph.

The importance of mentors is a recurring theme in my conversations with those at the top of their booze-soaked careers. I asked Joy what she learned from her predecessor.

"He taught me everything about rum blending, how to hone my sensory skills." Even more than that, she said, "I was actually able to combine art and science, because he was much more of an artist than a scientist, and I was able to combine the two."

I wondered what this combination looked like in practice. I had the image in my head of Joy—possibly in a cave of sorts—with a team of assistants, walking from barrel to barrel, smelling, tasting, swirling, making pronouncements. How did this incorporate her scientific training? Did this actually happen in a stainless steel cathedral?

It comes down to instinct and data, both, she said: "The artistry side is having that natural ability to understand how to blend different types of rum to create the blend of flavors that you desire in the particular expression that you're making. And then there's the chemistry aspect where you do the analysis on the rum and actually explore from a scientific perspective. When you have the scientific background and also the natural artistry, you're able to better understand the process and be able to perfect it somewhat." Having the experience to know how to mix flavors complements knowing what chemical compounds produce what aromas and how a rum's alcohol level will impact flavor. This and a thousand other small details, from the placement of barrels to the arrangement of molecules, between fermenting molasses and emptying barrels, make up the master blender's oeuvre.

Through this exuberant combination of art and science, she has been moving the company forward for over two decades—including a move into the premium spirits market with longer-age statement releases and limited bottlings. Premium spirits, the trade mags say, are the future. In 2017 Appleton released a twenty-five-year-old "Joy Blend," a limited edition bottling to honor Joy's twentieth anniversary in the top job. It was received to almost unanimous praise for its citrus, spice, and toasted almond notes and long, long finish. If anyone reading this wants to spend $250 on a gift for me, this would be it. I might even share some.

Back in reality, I really wanted to know what she looks for in a protégée. According to Joy, a STEM background is key, but there are other important aspects.

"If someone wants to actually enter the spirits industry or rum-manufacturing field, it's best to have a degree in chemistry or biochemistry, because the whole process of fermentation and distillation is science based. [They need] to be able to understand the process and to control the process. Then you also have to have strong natural sensory skills, because that's what you're actually going to use much more than any scientific training if you're going to taste all of your product and learn how to blend different aromas. Thirdly, you have to have a little bit of client skills, because now you actually become the face of the brand and you have to represent it globally. So you have to have some PR ability."

Beyond that, she says, to be the boss, you have to know how to think outside the box: "Look at other [manufacturing] processes as a mirror image, because you are always learning something in the industry. Always look to get new ideas and look at new processes, and know other people in the spirits world are looking at their processes and trying to improve them." Do not be afraid of innovation, in other words, while you keep your traditional flavor profile in mind.

So to whom does Joy look to inform her production process? "The Scotch Whisky Institute. I read their research papers because there are a lot of similarities between Scotch and rum in terms of components of the stills and processes. So I spend a lot of time looking at their data."

As with any leadership position, a master blender "should really have good people skills, because you have to be able to work with various persons throughout the organization, especially in the production area—to give advice in terms of process improvement or any development you really want to accomplish—and you have to be able to work with that team."

I began to feel bad for pestering her about how I could get her job, but after two decades at the top, did she see herself retiring any time soon, or would she keep going for another twenty years?

Joy laughed. "No, there comes a time when you have to call it quits and hand over to the next generation. When the time comes I will let go. I'll slow down, especially if I'm feeling exhausted with the various travel

If someone wants to enter the spirits industry or rum-manufacturing field, it's best to have a degree in chemistry or biochemistry, because the whole process of fermentation and distillation is science based.

schedules that come with doing global education classes all over the world. Whenever I get back I know it's time to spend time with my roses."

Joy is a keen gardener, it turns out, and her roses were looking spectacular. She talked to them regularly and they'd just bloomed beautifully. It makes sense now, the ad copy for the Joy Blend, for which she is quoted: "I simply set out to create the rum that I'd like to sip while watching the colors of my garden change in the warm glow of the Jamaican sunset." How appropriate, this deep appreciation for natural beauty. I saw the sugarcane grasses rippling, the cane juice dribbling out of a stalk with a glint. I saw the oak trees stippling the sunlight and smelled their woody vanilla aroma. I imagined microbes hard at work, gorging themselves on sugar to create this strange intoxicating compound. I imagined the culmination of all these things in a barrel, then a bottle, and it seemed perfect to have someone with a palate for beauty and a green thumb at the helm. I commented that this sounded like a relaxing pastime, and Joy responded, "Very relaxing. Especially when they start to bloom. Mine bloom large, magnificent blooms, and people ask, 'How come your roses look like that?' It's the love, all the love."

Brandy, You're a Fine Pour

If there is a spirit that gets the geek juices flowing as much as mezcal, it is brandy. It was the go-to spirit for Europe and its wealthier colonials until the Phylloxera aphid blight wiped out France's grape crops in the mid-1800s, after which Scotch whisky swooped in to fill up the void. Cognac has remained the province of high-class boozers, ballers, and Wisconsinites (Wisconsin is famously, mysteriously, the only place in the world where the old-fashioned has been made with brandy and lemon-lime soda for decades), but brandy as a whole is so much more.

Technically, any spirit made from the fermented juice of any fruit is classified as brandy. Just as "whisk(e)y" is the umbrella term for all brown liquor made from grains (i.e., Scotch whisky, Irish whiskey, Canadian whisky, bourbon whiskey), "brandy" is a far-reaching class of spirits that includes calvados (made from apples), cognac (grapes), slivovitz (plums), grappa (grape stems), and countless eaux-de-vie. Brandy can be aged or unaged and can come from pears, peaches, apricots, or cherries. If it sprouts from a plant and contains sugar, you can probably ferment and distill it. In the Austrian Alps, they make brandy out of pinecones. True story.

I would visit my family back home and see everyone drinking pisco. I always wondered: Why don't I see anyone drinking this beautiful, fun cocktail around the world?

Pisco is the unadulterated grape brandy made in the countries along the west coast of South America. Production dates back to the sixteenth century, and it is the national spirit of both Peru and Chile. Both countries claim national provenance and rights to the appellation. Peru's pisco, however, has always been my favorite, since the rules of its national denomination of origin make it a seriously interesting product. Peruvian pisco must be made from the fermented juice of a handful of grape varietals and distilled only once to proof. It cannot have any water added after distilling or be aged in any kind of wood, but it has to "rest" for at least three months in glass, concrete, or stainless steel containers that will not impart any additional flavors. There is no way to cover up low-quality raw materials or careless craft.

The Peruvian pisco sour—egg white, special limes, sugar, and pisco shaken to frothy bliss and served up with cinnamon-heavy bitters on top—has been an iconic cocktail for decades. Pisco punch (a pisco and pineapple drink) is less famous these days, but it was to gold rush–era San Francisco what the cosmopolitan was to 1990s New York.

Pisco caused one of my very first big spirit(ual) awakenings. First off, I've always been anomalously interested in the Andes, poring over textbook photos of Machu Picchu as a student, dreaming of the day when I could hike up those stone steps to the top of the world, lung capacity be damned. Before I was illicitly taking nips from $100 bottles of mezcal while bartending, I was a waitress sipping on pisco shift drinks. This fixation led eventually to a trip to Lima right at the beginning of my bar education. Dishing with Peruvian friends over coca-leaf-infused pisco sours at the Hotel Bolivar (amazing how those coca leaves improve one's Spanish), I knew I was in for it. I never made it to Machu Picchu but instead brought home well over the legal limit of Peru's national spirit, and was beyond satisfied.

For a few years now, the buzz in the cocktail community has been that it is pisco's time to emerge from obscurity and take the world by storm. Melanie Asher has been leading this charge for thirteen years. Melanie and her sister Lizzie co-own and operate Macchu Pisco, a brand that has grown large in a relatively small category, establishing itself as "the world's first super-premium pisco" and finding champions among the world's top bars and restaurants. In 2015 Melanie was awarded the Pioneer Award from Tales of the Cocktail's Dame Hall of Fame for her work spreading pisco awareness and her commitment to fair agricultural and production practices. I knew this before speaking with Melanie, who is based in Ica, Peru's pisco heartland, but what she told me changed my entire view of the category. Melanie Asher is on a crusade, and the fate of Peruvian pisco hangs in the balance.

The Asher sisters were born in Lima to a Peruvian mother and Brazilian father. They moved to Washington, DC, as children when their mother remarried an American, who became their adopted father. They never lost touch with their roots. "I would visit my family back home and see everyone drinking pisco," Melanie told me. The spirit barely existed in the United States then. "I always wondered: Why don't I see anyone drinking this beautiful, fun cocktail around the world?" It became her dream at the age of twelve to make pisco, and one she held on to through college, working on Wall Street, and attending Harvard Business School. "When I graduated I said, 'It's now or never to live out my dream,' and came with a backpack to the rural lands of Peru where I didn't know anybody." A self-proclaimed "DIY type" and a quick learner, Melanie soon found mentors and learned how to make wine and distill. "I'm basically a winemaker and a distiller and a blender."

From there, she enlisted her father to invest and soon secured investments to launch her dream company. Shortly thereafter Lizzie, an attorney, came on board. Melanie is CEO, in charge of production and other things; Lizzie is president, in charge of financials, among other things. A lot of things, it turns out. "Between the two of us, we wear all the hats," Melanie said. Even after thirteen years of producing and bottling, marketing, and being embraced by the global cocktail community, they have no other full-time employees. I complimented her on the exuberance of her web copy, which conveys a sense of adventure fitting the sweeping photoscapes of the Andes foothills. Melanie confirmed the brand is an extension of their personalities, their marketing "organically grown," as they haven't hired copywriters or found designers through personal contacts.

There is something unabashedly feminine and bold in the pictures of the Asher sisters in the photo archives for Tales of the Cocktail or various cocktail and charitable events. They have socialite smiles and buoyant fashion sense, and it would be tempting to discount their endeavor as a vanity project until you talk to them. Particularly now, Melanie's thoughts are hyperfocused on her product and how to preserve the four-hundred-year-old tradition to which she has dedicated her life.

"I've totally changed tack this year," she said, after the small talk was out of the way. "It's kind of serendipitous that you've called this moment... This year I was trying all my piscos, and it's taken so long for it to mature from last year." How does a product "mature" without barrel aging? We'll get to that.

"*Apuchado* [likely derived from the Peruvian slang *pucho*, meaning 'cigarette'] means you can taste the part of the tail that tastes like a burnt cigarette. Usually the smokiness dissipates...But now it's just stuck there." Though it had aged over a year, Melanie wouldn't bottle the liquid until it was ready. Lizzie, the numbers partner, was worried about running out of product, but the *distiladora* would not release an inferior product, because "the bartenders notice these things."

"I was like, 'What's wrong with this?'"

The Ica Valley is a key farming region that is in the middle of what Melanie calls an "agricultural boom." She elaborated: "The desert highlands in the Andes foothills have a perfect microclimate for pisco grapes: very hot during the day, cool at night," and near-equatorial sunshine without the heat or humidity of tropical climes. "It makes for a product available nowhere else in the world. The grapes have such high sugar content due to the climate," making them great for distilling, as more sugar equals more alcohol in the fermentation stage. In recent years, foreign interest in other kinds of Peruvian produce has escalated,

Melanie Asher
Photo Courtesy of Macchu Pisco

making it a huge exporter of asparagus and table grapes, which have also become prolific in the amenable climate. As a resident of California, I can't help seeing parallels to our own Central Valley. Reports come from the area now about clashes over groundwater and land rights between large industrial farms and smaller ones.

"Twelve years ago, there was no movie theater in the area," Melanie told me. "Lights were out at nine, because they were getting up at four A.M. to do the harvest. Now this agricultural boom has taken place. There is zero unemployment. People are migrating [here] to work." Farmworkers are not the only ones taking notice, unfortunately. Producers of agricultural chemicals, possibly driven by the rising demand for organic produce in the United States and Europe, have also flooded in.

Melanie pulls no punches when it comes to this issue, comparing the companies behind weed killers to drug pushers. "The first one is always free," she said, and soon, the idea of saving the 50 soles (about $15 USD) a day to hire someone to pull weeds seems like a needless expense. In a place where the "agro boom" has brought unemployment to basically nil, it's hard to find labor to begin with, and chemical sprays have become the norm.

"The peasant farmers have been bitten by greed and the lie of the companies...who say if you don't spray, the birds are going to eat your crops. To the point where I'm walking the grape fields and I'm finding dead birds." This is disturbing, but I wondered how the chemical sprays were affecting her pisco, exactly.

"I distill to proof," she said. "No one else in the world [besides pisco producers] distills to proof." Many producers have started illicitly diluting their pisco, according to Melanie. The reason for this is "when you have all these chemicals in the grape and then you ferment and distill, the tail, your tails, are going to be bringing a lot of these impurities from the grape."

Quick explanation (apologies if you're already familiar with the distilling process or couldn't care less): distillation comes in three stages. When heat is applied to a container of fermented grape juice, hypervolatile compounds known as the "heads," which include things like methanol

66

I distill to proof. No one else
in the world [besides pisco
producers] distills to proof.

99

that can be highly toxic, are the first to evaporate. Part of the distiller's job is to make sure these don't recondense into the final product, so she lets this first bit float off into the ether instead of trapping it to recondense and contaminate her liquor. At a certain point, the distiller "cuts," or starts collecting the good stuff, the "hearts"—these include that sweet, intoxicating ethyl alcohol and other flavorful but less harmful compounds—as the still heats up hotter. As it approaches the boiling point of water, she stops collecting the condensed goodies, this last bit called the "tails": less volatile stuff that evaporates at hotter temperatures, like water. This is how distilling transforms a 13 percent alcohol solution into a 40 to 60 percent alcohol solution; it leaves a big chunk of H_2O behind, along with some nastier-tasting stuff. It's also what makes pisco so tricky—the sooner you "cut" the tails, the stronger the brew, alcohol-wise, and the fewer unpleasant compounds make it in. Unlike most other spirits, pisco can run through the process only once and can't be watered down afterward. The distiller is much more limited in what she gets to omit from the final product. Read: your raw materials better be clean enough to eat. As Melanie put it, "Each bottle of Macchu Pisco can contain up to 1,000 grapes. Would you eat 1,000 grapes that have been sprayed? Doubt it."

"What [other distillers] do is they will end up cutting the body ["hearts"] higher and watering it down, which is another dirty secret." Adding water is prohibited by the denomination of origin, "which is something completely unique and crazy in the world. I've talked to Russians [making vodka] and they're like, 'How on earth do you distill to proof? That's insane.'"

Pisco hangs around in concrete or glass for a few months to a year, during which time, any lingering unpleasant flavors from the tails are supposed to mellow or dissipate on their own, allowing the fruit to shine through. If you've ever savored a really good pisco neat, you understand why producers take the trouble. It's an intense and complex liquor, with flavors that vary widely according to grape varietal, irresistible in a tart drink. This is the story of super-premium spirit: every piece of the process must be watched. Which, in Ica in the 2010s, is becoming next to impossible.

"When I started producing, the grape growers were not using pesticides because it was expensive. Just by default, everything was organic." Thirteen years in, Melanie faced a choice: "I could turn a blind eye and pretend everything was hunky dory, but I said, 'Something's not right here.'" She started talking to the farmers.

"It's been sad, I've actually had to break ties" with those who had turned to chemical agriculture. Melanie told other horror stories of unscrupulous pisco makers collecting damaged table grapes from vineyards producing for supermarkets and distilling these, completely contrary with the denomination.

Starting at the end of 2017, she announced the company's new direction: "*If you've already sprayed, you're out.* Which was heart wrenching, because I've been working with these farmers for ten years." Macchu Pisco had long touted its commitment to fair trade, particularly in supporting women growers. "It's just become something beyond gender. Are you doing what you know is right in your life? Are you being guided by intuition, or are you believing the lie?"

Melanie is a professed meditator, and her speech was peppered with lingo familiar to me as a Californian and dabbler in the whole mindfulness bag: "intent," "intuition," the focus on following the heart. I dug it but wondered about the practical aspects of keeping a business alive. As a result of this "new direction," her production dropped to 30 percent of what it was last year. "Because there's no such thing as organic grapes in Peru. [They do] not exist." She'd had to convince her investors and her co-owner/sister that this was the right thing for the company. "They're like, 'You're what? You're paying more for grapes and making less [pisco]?'" It's taken time, but she thinks her sister is coming around. It's a question of long-term survival. I got the distinct feeling that this was a woman who doesn't abide obstacles very long. She appeared to me adept at grinding down impediments, even by force of will.

Though cutting ties with long-term suppliers was hard, Melanie spoke with great enthusiasm. It truly felt like a quest.

"The barrier is 'no pesticides, no herbicides.' It's kind of a really cool project." She was pulling out some big philosophical guns to stay her course at this tenuous time. "I'm at the precipice right now; I don't know what's next. This is Macchu Pisco 2.0: making an all-natural product that starts with the raw material, because that works. Morality is utilitarianism. Because it really is what works. When you don't do what's right, it comes and bites you in the ass."

How did she plan to execute Macchu Pisco 2.0?

This year she's paying a premium to people who are doing things the old-fashioned way and checking to make sure they're following through. "People that are not using herbicides, their camps look really ugly. I found a snake in one of them the other day," she said with a laugh. "It's weeds up to your knees."

Of course, this type of vineyard biodiversity is precisely what Alice Feiring was looking for during her forays in France and Italy, checking out makers of "her" kind of wine, those that started with wild, untidy rows full of good microbe-friendly flora and fauna.

This concept that wine is made in the vineyard, not in the cellar or the lab, should be a familiar one if you read through chapter 1. It's no coincidence: in pursuing her Macchu Pisco 2.0 vision, Melanie sought out training in the same region that inspired winemaker Deirdre Heekin: Tuscany. Just before her pisco crisis came to light, she went to the university in Pollenzo, the birthplace of the slow food movement, where she got a certificate in "slow wine production."

"It's all been destiny or serendipitous, because I was there before I tried my pisco that wasn't maturing." The Pollenzo program's backbone is that raw material matters in the utmost, and "they're obviously against chemical farming." She visited natural winemakers in Italy, and even though she's been doing this for twelve years, took some cues from them in terms of the heat and length of her distilling process.

It is this flexibility that perhaps keeps Melanie going, allowing her to adapt to shifting environmental pressures. She admits that her philosophy has come a long way since the beginning. Coming out of business school, she said, she wanted to be "the next Diageo, the next Campari or Pernod Ricard, to start out with one brand and become multinational. I never imagined I would sell out to a big company, rather that I would become the big company." Instead, she finds herself preparing to drive eight hours outside of Ica on the intel that there is a farmer out there who leaves their grapes alone.

In addition to buying grapes only from personally verified organic growers, Melanie plans to work with the farmers and educate them on how to work organically. She is mindful of their livelihoods and is imparting many of the techniques she came by in Tuscany and elsewhere: getting the farmers access to good composts and biodegradable fertilizers, implementing other methods to scare away birds so they don't lose 30 percent of their grapes. Mold and fungus are a huge concern with grapes of any ilk, but "good" fungi can be used on grapes to combat harmful fungus. "It's working biodynamically to come up with how nature meets science." She started distilling her latest vintage two weeks ago, and she can already tell the product is coming out much better.

This is hopeful news. At this moment, Melanie's "precipice" seems all too real; she is looking at a massive loss of revenue this year but seems to have taken this as a necessary part of transformation. She remains optimistic: "There are still farmers that are doing what they know is right. And intuitively I've found old-school farmers that will say, 'Are you kidding me? I tried those pesticides and weed killers on one plant, and it debilitated the plant. The taste of the grape is not as good and the stalk is weakened.'"

All this considered, the product itself is bound to change. Macchu Pisco's flagship was previously made from 100 percent quebranta grapes, which she now reports have become too scarce to continue with this recipe. "Macchu Pisco will now become a blend in the field of all natural grapes. There's not enough good practice...to have enough of one varietal

I don't know what's going to happen, but I just have faith that things work out when you do what's right.

to have, say, an all-quebranta pisco. Instead of being grape-specific we're being farm-specific, of farmers who use good practices." Pisco in Peru is classified as *puro* (single varietal), *acholado* (blended varietal), or *mosto verde* (green must—distilled with residual sugar). For the first time in thirteen years, there will be no Macchu Pisco puro, but rather a guaranteed organic field blend, which to be honest, sounds downright cutting edge.

"I don't know what's going to happen, but I just have faith that things work out when you do what's right," she said, then drove it home: "I've crossed the Rubicon. I've burned a lot of bridges. I'm very confident in making a superior product that is made 100 percent naturally. There's not even one drop of water added."

Whisky Women Redux

Whiskey or whisky is one of the craft/locavore renaissance's biggest success stories, and it comes as no surprise that there are a lot of women out there shaking the trees in this area. For the purposes of this book, whiskey with an *e* is made in Ireland and the United States. Whisky with no *e* is made everywhere else. Don't ask me why; it's tradition, and it's not really important to me.

Before the resurgence of artisan gin, before rum became respectable, whisk(e)y was shaking off the dust, changing out of its frumpy suit, and coming into its own as a modern power player. In the late 1990s, bourbon nerds started a worldwide craze, Ireland went from having three domestic whiskey distilleries to almost thirty, rye came back from the dead as a cocktail staple, and Scotch...well, Scotch was always getting along just fine. Japanese distillers came up as the Hermione Grangers of the whisky world with their perfect single malts, and India's already robust domestic market went global. All over the world, the race was on to join the whisky boom.

France is known for many delicious things. Whisky is not one of them. When the Romans invaded Gaul in the first century BCE, they brought viticulture, and it stuck. When distilling technology migrated from the

Middle East, the French used it to distill wine into brandy, storing it in wood barrels that eventually became an essential part of the process in places like Cognac and Armagnac. The Brits, Scots, and Irish didn't have a grape-friendly climate, and they made their alcohol in the form of beer from cold-hardy barley. Eventually they distilled that beer into whisk(e)y and found success having perfected their own regional styles. Meanwhile, nobody went to the Continent for its single malts. Until now.

"Before launching my own whisky company," Allison Parc told me in between transatlantic flights, "I was a professional ballerina. I danced from nine years old to twenty-three." Allison is a thirty-something born and raised New Yorker. Her company, Brenne, produces single malt whisky from organic heirloom barley in Cognac, France. Since launching the label in 2012, she has achieved a loyal following among whisky fans.

It is interesting to note that Allison is not alone in transitioning from dance to booze. Deirdre Heekin and Alice Feiring, for instance, studied dance. I was a dance studio brat from kindergarten until my freshman year in college. Connection? Who knows. Perhaps a predilection for art and constant movement sets us up for nontraditional careers. When Allison stopped dancing at twenty-three, she was left casting around for a calling.

"I did some smaller jobs after that just to figure out who I was as an adult not in tights. I was a very late bloomer to the world of alcohol. All my friends had that college drinking experience and I missed that completely. Just being very seriously embedded in a profession where weight and physical appearance is a big part of what you do, as well as athletic ability. We [dancers] just really didn't drink."

Luckily, what she lacked in stories about vomiting cheap beer and Rumple Minze, she made up for in artistic sensibility and a profound appreciation for gustatory pleasures hitherto forbidden to her.

"When I got out [of ballet], I really fell in love with whisky, wine, and cheese." It was the early 2000s, the beginning of bourbon's mainstream revival, when rye was a bartender's secret handshake and Scotch was a

Allison Parc
Photo Courtesy of Brenne Whisky

"

I was asking people if
there were any single malt
whiskies that were evocative
of terroir—being of the earth.
At the time, there really
weren't people who were
having that conversation.

"

high roller's indulgence. As a young woman in New York, Allison felt somewhat baffled by the drinking scene. "This is the era of *Sex and the City*. Girlfriends would be out drinking cosmopolitans and talking about which character they really identified most with. But whisky—there were very few people drinking whisky. Whisky, for me, was really a big hook. It was all about the moment; it was the facilitator for incredible conversation, dropping into almost a mindfulness—dropping into the present moment. Whatever outfit I was wearing or what my hair looked like or who was I on a résumé, none of that mattered, and I just got to be me and that was enough. Not a lot of people in my age group were drinking whisky, so I was also hanging out with people of a different generation." She quickly found herself mesmerized by the conversation around terroir. Our old friend terroir. It never goes away, and for good reason.

Allison defines it this way: "'Terroir' is a word that is used throughout multiple regions of winemaking and it's all about being 'of the earth.' It's why a cabernet sauvignon from one side of the mountain tastes different from a cab sauv from the other, not only because of the winemaker's artistry but also because of sun exposure and mineral compounds or humidity levels or a microclimate on that side of the mountain." All of which is to say, "relating to the place in which it's made," all about the roots.

Soon she was investing more than time in her new obsession. "As a self-proclaimed whisky drinker, I was spending a lot of my money on beautiful single malts. Single malt was the style of whisky that really resonated with me."

"Single malt" refers to a style of whisky made from 100 percent malted barley (as opposed to rye, wheat, or corn like other kinds of whisky), made in a single distillery. A bottle of single malt might be a blend of liquid made in different years or aged in different barrels, but the main distinction is the singularity of ingredient and location. For Allison, this emphasis on location led to an obvious question: "I was asking people if there were any single malt whiskies that were evocative of terroir—being of the earth. At the time, there really weren't people who were having that conversation." Then she got her hands on some Yamazaki 18, a valuable eighteen-year-old Japanese single malt made by Suntory. That was her gateway whisky and she fell in love.

"It sent me down this exploration of single malt whiskies outside of Scotland, outside of Ireland." The Yamazaki's flavor was so unique compared with similar aged whiskies from Scotland that it pushed the terroir question further. She wanted to see if people could "experiment with using ingredients local and indigenous to our distillery's location, to effectively see if terroir can be experienced through the end product." Typically the idea that you can taste the place of origin in a liquid or a cheese applies to fermented products, not distilled spirits, which go through an extra layer of processing to concentrate the alcohol. Wine and cheese retain the by-products of the microbial processes that transform them. Still, terroir is a concept with a shifting definition, and Allison took it upon herself to satisfy her curiosity.

This was the start of a journey, though Allison was hard-pressed to explain how it all happened step by step. "When you're in it, it doesn't seem so clear."

She was in it, and at the time, she said, her "life looked like a giant hairball."

"I can stand here today and look backwards and be like this is what happened and then that happened, and then that happened and that door opened, and that's how I have a whisky company." In retrospect, sure.

At first, she wasn't planning on making the stuff; she just wanted to find it. She set up an import company and focused on world (non-Scotch, non-Irish) whiskies that had a strong connection to the land. The problem was: there weren't any. She began a blog called the *Whisky Woman* to connect to other drinkers and find what she was looking for.

"[Whisky and terroir] made really a happy marriage in my brain, and since we couldn't really find any on the market, I thought that that was a shame. I thought that it could be done." After researching the market, she settled on France. Why France? First, it already had a strong distilling tradition with brandy. But mostly, the country was the birthplace of appellations, the sense that an agricultural product is and should be defined by the place it comes from.

"You think about France, you think about terroir. You think about their wines, their cheeses. Everything has a sense of place designated by the earth, by the earth's goodness. You have calvados, cognac, and armagnac with these really rich distillation histories within France. Yet no one was making a French single malt whisky."

I commented how that was curious, as it's not like there is a shortage of grains in France.

Allison was right there with me, extending the terroir theme even further: "Exactly. You eat a croissant from France versus a croissant from the US and it's a totally different ball game. Their grain and their water sources just do something that's magical." She laughed.

Allison set out to find her distiller in the land of croissants. At first, the stillhouses were not having it. She was turned down over and over. Finally, "I partnered with this incredible family that's been making cognac since 1920. They're based in Cognac, France, which is in the middle of the country all the way over on the west coast. They have a cognac house. They make cognac; that's really their bread and butter. On the side, they started working with me to make this French single malt."

Even better, this distillery was focused on the craft of its production, rather than marketing a brand: "They don't bottle cognac under their own name. There's not a name on their distillery. They keep really quiet. They're a farm distillery." It was run by the founder's grandson, with whom Allison said she has a kind of sibling relationship. "We love each other and we definitely get on each other's nerves."

I asked if it took time to trust each other's tastes.

"Yes and no. He and I worked really, really hard...He thought I was crazy when I kept leaving the whisky in the barrel." Having studied whisky markets, particularly for single malts, Allison knew well the demand for high-age statements. "He still sometimes fights me when I'm like, 'No, we're leaving those [barrels]. I want to see what they'll taste like in fifteen years. I want to see what they'll taste like in twenty years.' He's like, 'Allison, I don't think that is the right thing. I think this is good now. I don't know why you won't pull it.' I'm like, 'Cool. I get that and you're right. We could lose that whisky if it doesn't continue to trend well." But still, she held firm to let the whisky age, saying, "We've got to find out."

When she started working with her French partners, they had in-house whisky made from local barley that was already between one and four years old and were pulling it out of the barrels relatively young. In the high-end whisky game, time is money, for real. As a lover of eighteen-year-old Yamazaki, Allison's intuition likely told her the wait would be worth it, despite her partners' impatience. Unless you are one of today's mad scientist distillers, bombarding your barrels with sonic waves or steeping wood chips or dust in your whisky, there is a depth of flavor and complexity that only comes with time. The astronomical prices of twenty-plus-year bourbons such as Pappy Van Winkle have proved that foresight and patience can pay off for a producer. Whisky, which comes off the still as a caustic, high-proof moonshine, picks up its brown color, round edges, and flavors such as vanilla, caramel, and baking spice from the barrel. It's a fascinating process, an infusion of wood into the liquid like tea. The longer you wait, the more of those sugars, tannins, and other compounds find their way from the wood into the whisky. In wine, many argue that wood interferes with terroir, but for whisky, where the wood accounts for about 70 percent of the flavor, one could argue that the barrel is what connects the whisky to the earth, even more than the grains from which it was made.

The result of her searching and haggling was Brenne whisky, a dark amber liquid somewhat lighter and sweeter than your average Speyside Scotch, a bit brighter and fruitier than most Irish whiskies, and, most important, something that tastes like itself. Allison described it as "elegant, rich, saturated in incredible fruit flavors, crème brûlée, bananas foster." The tasting notes were making me salivate. She talked about the whisky's approachability, how it is a nice entry point for the whisky novice. Personally, I find it a lovely summertime dram.

Her imagery bore this out: "It almost feels like a French picnic to me," she said, laughing. "You can get a visual and you're on the seaside—there's seagrass next to the ocean—on a sand dune, and it's just so beautiful. The linen napkins and the beautiful food and the baguette and everything." This Riviera holiday scene reveals the other secret of Brenne's success: Allison is hardworking and relentlessly charming. "Nothing has to be perfect. I don't have to be perfect. I don't have to fluff the pillows that I'm sitting on."

We both laughed at this. It would seem pretentious if she wasn't so excited and clearly cognizant of how ridiculous, but fitting, it is to pin such emotion to a beverage.

Having tasted the end product, I wanted to know more about how she got there. Whisky, by nature, is a waiting game. New whiskey distillers in Ireland and the United States, for example, have frequently sold vodka and gin while waiting for their stocks to mature—the constantly occurring word when talking about aged spirits. How many years until your product matures? How long can you afford to wait?

"This family [in Cognac] had actually started making a version of whisky that eventually became some of my early releases for Brenne. When I met them, they had been making a version of this whisky as their house spirit." I could only assume that "house spirit" meant the booze they drank at home, when not indulging in their pricey brandy. "They'd already started making something like this using two heirloom varietals of barley that they grew organically. They were fermenting it with their own strain of yeast and distilling in their alembic still, which is a typical cognac still." Great start for a craft spirit, no one can deny.

"When I met them, they actually had whiskies in the barrel that were four years old, three years old, two years old, one year old. I worked with them for another four years to bring those whiskies, the oldest ones, up to eight [years], and then we started bottling those in 2012."

While Allison kept close tabs on how the whisky was "coming together in the barrel," there were other bridges to be crossed. "It took us eleven years to make a ten-year-old whisky. It literally takes that time. I did a lot of odd things in the meantime." She quit her day job in 2010 to "give [herself] some time." Time for what? I wanted to know. If she quit her job two years before bottling her first batch, what went on in the interim?

"I really worked all 2011, most of 2012, on creating infrastructure for the business and learning the industry, because I'd never worked in this industry before. I hadn't even temped; I hadn't even bartended. I didn't inherit this business from my family. No one in my family works in this industry. I really had to learn every single thing from the ground up."

Learning the ins and outs in a few years of a centuries-old business such as the whisky trade could seem impossible. But Allison had one key advantage: "Coming from the world of ballet, which is so detail-oriented, so all about sacrifice, and so rigid in the fact of...none of this comes easy for you. With that lens, I felt like I had a good set of tools to just create a business inside an industry that I've never worked. That did not seem daunting to me. I was like, 'I get it. I just have to work really hard, I just have to learn.'" She read books, interviewed people, asked questions. Whatever it took to learn "every corner of this business...I learned about freight containers and longshoremen and shipping, down to the whisky making, down to barrel, down to negotiating for wood and international tariffs, and shipping logistics in the US, and taxes. Even how to source cork for the tops of your bottles, how to source glass, how to source labels."

So many of the success stories I'd learned about included a mentor or mentorship organization. I asked if there was any person or professional body that helped her gain this knowledge along the way.

"While I have been a one-person company since inception, people have always helped me out. I can't even point my finger and say this one person or this one group. Whisky collectors have been amazing and incredible supporters. We joke on Twitter and Instagram. We call it the 'Whisky Fabric.' There's just these incredible people all over the world who really, really love whisky...people in the industry who I've called out of the blue and been like, 'Hi. I'm trying to do this. Can I have an hour of your time?' People would really, really help me out. For sure, it was a fascinating time for me to experience that generosity from strangers."

"

I worked all 2011, most of 2012, on creating infrastructure for the business and learning the industry, because I'd never worked in this industry before. I hadn't even temped; I hadn't even bartended. I didn't inherit this business from my family. No one in my family works in this industry. I really had to learn every single thing from the ground up.

"

Reading through Allison's blog archive, it is clear. During this time, waiting to see what her malt would become, she was gathering a community around her. From the outset, TheWhiskyWoman.wordpress. com was a platform for her to share and gather knowledge, to make friends and give shout-outs, to log notes on whiskies she loved and post pictures from events. She had all the advantages of being a New Yorker, being conventionally attractive, having the confidence that comes with a background of performing, and she used all of this, along with persistence, intelligence, and work ethic, to build her brand, despite frequently being the only woman in the room. We talk a lot about privilege these days, usually in a negative way, but I see Allison's story as someone seeing the privilege she has and using it to overcome that which she doesn't, which has to be worth noting. If one barrier falls, we know it is possible. At least, that's what we hope. By her accounts, the overwhelmingly male whisky community online and in the real world were also largely supportive, particularly compared to the dance world, where people would "not want to share information for fear of being at a disadvantage." This is another thing that comes up repeatedly—from Teri Fahrendorf and others—that once you begin to talk shop with enthusiasts, bias frequently falls by the wayside. At the end of the day, we are all nerds. We just need to have access to the conversation.

In 2012, Allison was riding a Citibike around Manhattan with a box of Brenne bottles in the front basket, making deliveries to her first customers. More than six years later, Brenne whisky has received multiple awards for both content and representation, including two Icons of Whisky awards to Allison as Best Brand Representative. The distinct tall, slim bottle with the light blue label graces the shelves of bars and shops in thirty-five US states and three countries.

So what about being the only woman in the room?

"Being in the arts or being in ballet, it's so dominantly female." Even after becoming a prominent whisky blogger, "it never crossed my mind to even look at...gender ratios specifically in the whisky industry. It was only once I launched. I launched October 1, 2012, and I started doing tasting events and people would come to me and point to me. They were like, 'You're different.'"

Standing out in a growing field isn't always a bad thing, but being constantly reminded of your loner status gets a bit old. "They would tell me, 'Look around the room. You're the only woman here. You're the only woman representing her own brand. You're the only woman who has a brand right now. You're different. You're different. You're different.'"

Having taken years to educate and immerse herself in the Whisky Fabric, ,this singling out was somewhat unexpected: "It was the consumers and the media who were telling me how much of an anomaly I was, based on my gender, which has been a strange thing," she added. Strange, because as a start-up with no budget for marketing and relying on word of mouth, media attention was always welcome. Still, being known largely as the "ex-ballerina who makes the whisky" doesn't exactly advance her terroir-ist ideals. "If I had been a man, no one would've been talking about what I did before. Everyone would've been talking about what was amazing and technically different and interesting and award winning about my whisky. That wasn't the narrative and that was not what got shared. I just got [interviewed for] an article recently that was like, ' We're talking about terroir.' I was like, 'Oh, thank God.'"

As much as she would like to control the narrative around Brenne, Allison is pragmatic. "At the end of the day, people are going to create their own stories and draw their own parallels. I can only be me, I can only show up as authentic me in every given moment."

When Brenne launched in 2012, Japanese single malts had just crested into view on the mainstream US consciousness. "People getting their minds around the idea that award-winning whiskies can come from places outside of Scotland was absolutely paramount to the doors being more open to Brenne, to this French single malt that's being hauled around and delivered by bicycle by this crazy ex-ballerina." She laughed at this and said, *"What?"* as in *Who, me?*

A big help in the effort to get Brenne on shelves? Supporters in the whisky and bar communities—her "Brenne Boosters." All this work

> **"**
>
> *If I had been a man, no one would've been talking about what I did before. Everyone would've been talking about what was amazing and technically different and interesting and award-winning about my whisky.*
>
> **"**

also led to a transition from a lone-lady operation to Brenne joining the portfolio at the spirits company Samson & Surrey, which promotes and distributes craft brands from around the country. "They're this collective of a very tight-knit group of craft brands. It's FEW Spirits, Widow Jane, Bluecoat gin, and then Brenne. There are four Brennes right now. We'll probably go up to six total."

She had only nice things to say about her infrastructure company: "They're really fair and kind, and they value a certain quality in the way that they live, in the way that they carry themselves, in the ethos that they create in this company. Samson & Surrey is building out their sales teams, their marketing teams, their brand advocacy teams, and then these incredible humans that are living all over the country become the amplifiers for my voice.

"We definitely have incredible salespeople in the markets who are female and advocacy people in the markets who are female, but at the top level—at the management, at the director level, at the CEO level, at the presidential level, at the shareholder level—I have to pause and take note that wow, I'm the only woman at this table, I'm the only woman sitting at all those levels."

I asked her if she felt intimidated by this imbalance.

"God, no. Are you kidding? I'm one of the cofounders on the Fédération du Whisky de France, which is an organization in France to pull all the French whisky distillers together. I sat there on the very first day of when we started this organization in Paris and I didn't even speak French fluently. I was one of three women in a room of fifty, and two of them were assistants. I was the only woman at the table with a vote; I was the only woman at the table with a say in anything. Strangely, I was also the only American, and many times, I'm the only millennial.

"I think that's very important in the possibility of opening the door for more women, more millennials, and more minorities in the room."

In 2016, *Vice* media's *Munchies* site ran a piece claiming "just 12 people in the world hold the title of master whisky blender," a job that, if you read the rum chapter, you know is the supreme melding of artist and scientist, the boss of bosses who decides what a company's final product will taste like. Among this keen-nosed group was Rachel Barrie, the world's first woman master blender of Scotch whisky.

Ten years after Joy Spence first landed the chief chemist gig at Appleton Estate, Rachel received her chemistry degree from the University in Edinburgh. Rachel grew up in Aberdeenshire, an area east of the Scottish Highlands known for agriculture, natural gas, and being the site of the British royal family's vacation castle. She reported a lifelong appreciation for whisky, inherited from her grandmother who used to sneak her nips of the stuff when she was sick.

Despite being a whisky drinker, Rachel had initially imagined herself working in perfume or oil and gas. At that time she didn't see malt whisky as a welcoming place for women. However, after a year studying the chemistry of brewing, she won a prestigious internship with the Scotch Whisky Research Institute, in the process discovering she had an extremely sharp sense of smell. A true academic, once she knew she had the talent, she was bent on developing it.

In a piece for *Forbes* magazine in 2015, Rachel likened using her olfactory gifts to blend whisky to being a musician: something she might have an innate talent for, which she must hone through practice and study in order to become a "composer." This is a fascinating analogy, particularly having the insight of other master blenders on the equal importance of training, knowledge, and intuition in the role. From her internship she secured a blender position at the Glenmorangie distillery.

Rachel not only broke the glass ceiling when she became a whisky blender in 1995, but according to Fred Minnick's *Whiskey Women*, she revolutionized the job itself, doing "things that nobody had ever attempted in creating some of the best whiskies known to man." These things included changing up the types and ratios of malted barley used, aging in combinations of sherry, rum, and bourbon barrels, and blending very old whiskies with younger ones for totally new flavor profiles. Becoming the Glenmorangie master blender in 2003, she helped revitalize the portfolio at Ardbeg when her company acquired the Islay brand in the mid-2000s. During her tenure, Ardbeg became a cult favorite in the bar and whisky communities. Whither Rachel Barrie goes, accolades follow.

After seven years, Rachel left Glenmorangie and Ardbeg to head up operations at Morrison Bowmore's three distilleries, producing brands including Bowmore, Auchentoshan, Glen Garioch, and McClelland's. There she continued to innovate, using her by then fully honed sensory skills to make award-winning whiskies for each brand. She also became the public face of the company, traveling all over the world to hold tastings and trainings. Rachel's reputation had always been solid, but it was during these years with Bowmore that she truly became an industry star.

The experience with Ardbeg had given Rachel a taste of bringing a smaller brand out of obscurity, building it up and making it a mainstay. This is the experience she hoped to replicate in her latest position as the master blender for the BenRiach group. In 2016, American whiskey giant Brown-Forman made a return to the Scotch market when it acquired the group, which includes the Glenglassaugh, Glendronach, and BenRiach distilleries. Shortly after the buyout, Brown-Forman brought Rachel on to head the portfolio. The months after her hire, she described to whisky writer Giles Milton, were a deep dive into these three very different facilities, tasting whiskies up to fifty years in age, seeing what the inventory offered. BenRiach, in particular, had an extensive history to work with. Rachel's public attitude about it all was unrestrained enthusiasm, a total readiness to "take a distillery and make it the pinnacle, revered around the world."

Reminiscent of her friend Joy Spence, she added, "I would say my work is more art than science these days. Science is understanding nature; science is the theory. It is the start of your education, where you try to understand what's happening. I've tasted 150,000 casks, and once you have that understanding and that programming in your brain, it becomes intuitive."

The master blenders in this book are all icons—not in the least because they all represent a first in their fields. Taken together, they stand out as exceptional scientists as well as especially driven, bold, and hardworking people, committed to the idea that whatever they did not already know they could learn. When we talk about unfair hiring practices—whether the culprit be race, gender, religion, or sexual orientation—it's almost always true that the exceptions, those who do rise to the top despite conscious or unconscious bias, have worked three times harder to achieve their successes. It is much to their employers' benefits that they hired the first women master blenders or distillers in their fields, since the women with enough fortitude, intelligence, and drive to even be considered were more akin to forces of nature.

Gin Girls

I first met Natasha Bahrami when I was researching a freelance piece on barrel-aged gin. Early on in my freelance life, I wrote about whatever I was obsessed with at the moment: barreled gin, pine brandy, obscure liqueurs made from tree saps. Being enthusiastic about things that are particularly niche gives you an advantage: the experts you contact for quotes will be extra excited to share their wisdom.

So it was with Natasha, the self-proclaimed "Gin Girl" of St. Louis, owner and operator of the Gin Room bar. Having been put in touch by mutual friends, I was overwhelmed by her energy and focus.

"Gin has a multifaceted character that allows it to mold and bend and excite," she told me during that first interview. She went on to explain how gin, as a category, has a wider flavor range than spirits such as whisky, which is broken into categories with very specific regulations. It is true: gin, known as "mother's ruin" during the eighteenth-century English gin craze, a period when increased consumption of cheap grain alcohol was seen as a dire threat to female virtue, is largely what you make it. According to the US Alcohol and Tobacco Tax and Trade Bureau (TTB), gin is a neutral spirit flavored with botanicals, predominantly juniper. How these botanical flavors get there is a matter of taste and tradition.

Natasha Bahrami
Photo Credit: Tuan Lee

Following on whisky's heels, gin was primed for a comeback with the rise of the classic cocktail. Before Prohibition, gin was the clear liquor of choice, starring in such classics as the Martinez, the bijou, and the aviation. Vodka in the nineteenth century had the whiff of poverty and foreignness and, anyway, brought no flavor of its own to a cocktail. As bar nerds around the country started tracking down vintage cocktail books at the turn of the twenty-first century, they found that gin, along with rye whiskey, was indispensable.

Distillers responded with exuberance. Many who had set out to make whiskey found they could use their stills for clear spirits while the brown ones aged. Intrepid souls forsook the juniper-heavy London Dry style and made gins that tasted like orange, coriander, lavender, and saffron. Gin was back in. Or so it seemed, in the bubble of the cocktail community. In the wider populace, drinkers accustomed to extra-dry vodka martinis (read: *I'd like to get drunk quickly, please, and taste nothing*) would take some hard convincing that gin was more than a pine-flavored summer drink for the elderly. The person for this job was Natasha Bahrami.

Although she always knew that she would be a part of the restaurant business, Natasha's entry into the spirits world was comparatively recent. Her parents, Hamishe and Behshid Bahrami, immigrated to the United States from Iran in the 1970s and started a luncheonette with a convection oven and an electric burner in a downtown St. Louis office building, serving standard American comfort food with the occasional Persian touch tucked in. Business was steady, and as years passed they introduced more flavors from home to the palates of their Budweiser-and-bratwurst Midwest city. Ten years later they opened Cafe Natasha, a sit-down restaurant specializing in Middle Eastern cuisine. Natasha was eleven years old when her parents named their restaurant after her and is quick to point out that it was not her decision. The restaurant is a staple in St. Louis.

I had just seen her in New Orleans, and she'd recently done a run of events in the UK. She told me about the turning point in her culinary career. After graduating college, she was living in Washington, DC. She could not tell me at what bar or what gin it was, but she clearly remembers the drink that brought on her gin obsession: a dirty martini.

(Now I know plenty of cocktail nerds who scoff at the use of olive brine, but personally I think this is nonsense. We love shrubs. We salinate savory drinks. Vinegar is vinegar, salt is salt, and a well-mixed blend of gin, vermouth, and olive brine can, in fact, be delicious.)

What caught her attention was the multifaceted flavor, the combination of savory and sharp and herbaceous. After discovering the possibilities in gin, Natasha said she "went down the rabbit hole." She spent three more years in DC, immersing herself in cocktail culture, homing in on the demographic. When she returned to St. Louis, she converted half of Cafe Natasha into a gin-centric cocktail bar with an emphasis on consumer education.

"Despite what everyone said, that it was a niche category," she said, talking about this time, "worst-case scenario: I'd have a lot of gin at my disposal." The finished Gin Room had around three hundred pouring gins, plus special tasting-only bottles that weren't licensed for sale in Missouri. Her cocktail menu was built on each gin's specific profile, so if the gin were switched out, the recipe wouldn't work. She wanted to illustrate to her community the variety she'd fallen for. This was in 2014. There was already a craft cocktail scene in St. Louis, but gin was (and is) still behind brown spirits in popularity. But Natasha knew her community and her product, and she had faith, saying, "Sometimes people tell you no, and if you have a lot of love and passion, you keep going."

She kept going. She hired bartenders with equal fervor for their product. She held tastings, blogged as the "Gin Girl." She went to trade events and made friends. In short: Natasha worked it. Of course, having the support of her family and community was huge.

"Without Cafe Natasha and my family business, the Gin Room would in no way have been able to do what it's been able to do in such a short period of time," she said. "It's because of the trust that the community already had with us that we were allowed to engage that audience. I couldn't have done it as a stand-alone, not as quickly as we did." The trust

Sometimes people tell you no, and if you have a lot of love and passion, you keep going.

she and her family had earned over thirty years helped her push on with her agenda of gin-lightenment.

The first time I visited the bar, a few months after our initial interview, Natasha made me a martini with a gin she had just gotten in that she was excited about. I'm not usually a martini drinker, as I find it's so difficult to make them balanced that I don't want to risk it. But her choice of Eden Mill's Love Gin, with its subtle floral notes and silky texture, and the exact right vermouth, garnished with a rose petal, just slayed me. I remember thinking, *If this woman can't make you love gin, you probably have no soul.*

A year after opening the Gin Room, Natasha needed more. It was all well and good to teach about gin from her little corner of St. Louis's University Loop, but she was trying to start a movement. In 2015, she organized the annual St. Louis Gin Festival—the largest of its kind in the United States—featuring educational and drinking events in local bars and restaurants. Distillers were invited to bring their bottles, to hold events at local venues, and to talk directly to consumers. Working with a small team, she did it again in 2016. Then, as she told me that fall, she was poised to go global. By 2017, she had almost single-handedly organized Gin World, a series of educational events followed by citywide Gin Festivals in St. Louis, DC, San Francisco, and New Orleans (at Tales of the Cocktail) and in the United Kingdom n.

I asked her what she hoped to achieve through all this organizing, and Natasha spoke with intensity: "Gin World is absolutely education focused, and it is focused not only on gin enthusiasts, but those who have no idea and those who are just curious and those who don't like gin at all. It's catering to all those demographic bases and really geared to increase curiosity about the range and spectrum of the spirit." This made sense. The more people came to like gin, the better for business. But her interest in building the community was equally as urgent. "There are many people in this world who have positioned themselves to be advocates of certain spirits categories. When I meet them, we have so much in common, because we are dedicating our lives to something and to people who don't really have an understanding of what we're working with. And it's fun, because most of our successes come from meeting people who are like, 'I don't like this spirit at all,' and really getting them to not necessarily love it, but to understand its breadth. That's what we're doing and that's why it was so important to take it away from...my hometown, because although the festival continued to grow, there was a massive limitation on who we were reaching and the spectrum of brands and spirits we were able to work with." Since liquor licensing laws vary dramatically between states, some spirits can be popular in one region and unheard of in others. "That's what makes Gin World different. It's not limited to what we are allowed to legally use in St. Louis, Missouri. It expands the spectrum so that I can work with craft brands or big brands from all over the world, [which] allows it to be less about the specific brands and more about... show[ing] off the spectrum of gin."

I asked her how many events she'd put on so far.

"If I put a count I'd say maybe 110 events...DC was 45 events not counting Gin Festival, St. Louis was 43 events not counting Gin Fest, then you can count England and New Orleans and now we're going into San Francisco, so yeah! It's definitely been a busy year, but I think we made the progress that we tried to do in a very short period of time."

Building a "gin community" was definitely high on her priorities list. When we spoke about how she initially immersed herself in the spirits world, she said her colleagues were among the best resources. "We have a strong spirits community, and all of us, each and every one of us, has helped uplift each other. That's been really exciting to see. From those of us who run gin bars to those who write about gin, to judging for spirits competitions, we all seem to be in this together, and the growth of one of us is the growth of all of us." It's that collaborative, rising-tide sentiment that has become a familiar refrain among minority communities within the spirits business. The "minority," in this case, just happens to be gin lovers.

2017 was a productive year for Natasha but not an easy one. In December 2016, her father, Behshid, passed away, mourned by the entire St. Louis restaurant community. Natasha's plans for Gin World moved forward, but

We have a strong spirits community, and all of us, each and every one of us, has helped uplift each other. That's been really exciting to see. From those of us who run gin bars to those who write about gin, to judging for spirits competitions, we all seem to be in this together.

watching her go, go, go on social media caused me a prickle of concern. In 2018, she refocused on her most successful events in Washington, DC, and St. Louis and appeared to have slowed the roll a little. "Life is...it's like . . . even when you had two weeks of downtime, it's like *no! Not really.* But everything's okay. We're just getting through this life, that's all. I'm fine and we are moving forward and gin is taking over the world. So that's what our goal is."

Just taking over the world, is all.

Melissa Katrincic's name rhymes with "intrinsic." It was the first thing I asked her when I got her on the phone. Her maiden name was Green. "That's commitment," I said. This made her laugh.

"It's lucky I still like him after seventeen years," she said.

I'd met Melissa at Natasha Bahrami's Gin World tasting in New Orleans during Tales of the Cocktail, when she offered me a taste of her Conniption American Dry and Navy Strength gins, part of a line of gins and liqueurs from Durham Distillery in North Carolina. Melissa and her husband Lee founded the distillery in 2013, rooted in their science backgrounds and driven by her love for gin.

The distillery embraces traditional methods as well as innovative ones, an ethos evident right down to their tagline: "Traditional Spirits of the New South." Gin is essentially neutral spirit with fragrant plants infused, macerated, and/or redistilled in to provide that herbaceous element. Originally, this made terrible booze more palatable and transformed traditional herbal medicines into quaffable drinks. Today, gin is made in a variety of ways. One of the more traditional methods involves suspending a basket of botanicals in the still to infuse the rising alcohol vapor as the distiller turns up the fire under the pot. This works well for heartier plants like juniper, but doesn't allow delicate, heat-sensitive herbs to shine. Modern distillers get around this conundrum by using a technique called vacuum distillation. I like to think of this method as using science to "science" the vapors through the botanicals at room temperature, capturing a lot of nuanced goodness along the way. It's a fascinating process, one that should definitely be explored in detail on a distillery tour in Durham, NC, where Melissa and Lee employ both methods to layer their Conniption gins with enchanting flavors.

After three years in business, Durham Distillery has become a presence in the global gin community, being recently inducted into the international Gin Guild—one of only a handful of American brands to do so.

Much like the husband and wife team behind Benchmark Brewing that we met in the beer chapter, Melissa handles the marketing and brand administration, while Lee does the distilling. She had over a decade of experience in marketing, while Lee worked as a pharmaceutical chemist. Her lifelong interest in gin inspired her to convince Lee that this fascinating and divisive spirit was their future.

As a microdistillery limited by capacity and the arcane systems of state-by-state and international alcohol distribution regulations, Durham needed all the help it could get to spread the word. Melissa and Lee knew their product spoke for itself, but getting it into the right hands would take some work. This was where Gin World came in.

When I spoke to Melissa in New Orleans, she'd been giving tastings of her products for more than two hours. It was a large, convention-like event, with distillers, distributors, and brand heads arrayed in a large oval of tables decorated to show off their wares, handing out samples to those who wandered in. This was a ticketed event for the bartending community but free to the press. One highly suspicious thing about most of Tales's tastings, from my point of view, is that there are no spittoons to be found. I became a little bit of an anomaly by carrying an extra paper cup with me to expel spirits after I'd held them on my tongue for a few seconds. As you can probably imagine, the events get increasingly rowdy as the days go on. At this time, it was about 4:00 P.M. I'm certain at least half the convention was three sheets to the wind. It impressed me how cool and patient Melissa and her cohorts remained.

Melissa told me that the frenetic atmosphere at these events was nothing but encouraging. She mentioned how one of her associates had represented Durham at the Gin World tasting in DC: "She said she never had a moment to herself, which is what you want in those events, right? You want to be overrun with people. Honestly, when the tasting room started winding down we were complaining because we could've gone for at least another two hours."

I most definitely did not want to see what the influencers would have looked like after another two hours. But she was correct: for a small company, this time was crucial.

"One of the things that I admire about Natasha and Jen [Gregory, Natasha's right hand in New Orleans] and what they have put together with Gin World is that they're not trying to have it be all of the [brands] that you already know. Especially for us, we are two years in the market at the end of this month, and a big portion with my background being a marketer is trying to efficiently build awareness. Because we just can't afford media right now. It's about reaching the right people who are interested in the gin community. [We've had] really amazing growth within the last eighteen months, and so when Natasha decided to go ahead and do Gin World in cities other than St. Louis, we immediately said yes. Because we knew that was going to be where our customers were and we were going to be able to efficiently reach them and have them taste the product. It's not just about the reviews and it's not just about hearing about us; it's about that face-to-face time."

It is this confluence of makers and enthusiasts that make these brands come to life. I asked Melissa how she and Lee heard about Gin World to begin with.

"Within the gin community, the same as in the whisky community, you get to know who the movers and shakers are. When you start to get involved in the influencer community, you make sure that you know exactly what's going on and where you can be a part of it." In other words, passion for your product is key, but so is awareness of your market and the chutzpah to knock on some doors.

At this writing, Conniption gins are available in North and South Carolina, Georgia, and Washington, DC. Despite this relatively small

"

Within the gin community, the same as in the whiskey community, you get to know who the movers and shakers are. When you start to get involved in the influencer community, you make sure that you know exactly what's going on and where you can be a part of it.

"

distribution area, the Katrincics have received stellar reviews from national websites. They continue to hit the conventions to get the word out, including Junipalooza, the largest gin show in the world, put on each year in London by the brains behind the Gin Foundry website. The festival coincides with World Gin Day, the second Saturday in June.

"There are usually right around fifty gin distillers. We were one of only four distillers from the US invited to go to it this year; it was quite an honor. It [runs for] two days: two sessions on Saturday that are at least four hours long, and then a session on Sunday which is five hours long, and I will tell you Lee and I spoke to over three thousand people at this event. It was a whirlwind. But those kinds of events for the gin community are critical. So I'm just really excited that Natasha is trying to get these going consistently in the US." She pointed out that though it has grown drastically in popularity in the past decade, American gin drinkers are not yet pulling their weight. "We're behind in this country. I think any gin distiller will admit that to you. We're behind where the UK especially is. I have the—for lack of a better word—I have the double penalty of being focused on gin and being in the American South where bourbon is king. So for me, I'm like, *This is fantastic!*"

I hadn't thought about this, trying to sell clear spirits in the birthplace of the mint julep. Melissa shows no intention of compromising her commitment to the spirit she loves. "We are through and through a gin distillery. That's our goal. We've got really big plans, and so having an advocate like Natasha is helpful for all of us to rise together."

Of the brand's future, there is no hesitation: "When anyone thinks of craft gin in the South, we want them to think of Conniption."

England is gin's homeland and therefore has a long history making the spirit. One of the UK's oldest continuously operating gin producers is G&J Distillers, previously known as G&J Greenall, the makers of the 250-year-old Greenall's gin brand. In 2006, Joanne Moore became the first woman master distiller at G&J and by most accounts the first female master gin distiller in the world. Like other first ladies profiled here, Joanne began her career with a degree in biochemistry and became an "accidental distiller" after being hired to work in the G&J quality control lab in 1996. So it goes with these hyperintelligent, hypercreative individuals: after being promoted to quality manager, Joanne developed a talent for blending botanicals and started working closely on brand development with the master distiller at the time. The seventh person to hold the title in the company's history, Joanne is known across the spirits world for creating brands including Berkeley Square, BLOOM, Thomas Dakin, and Opihr gins. Each of these has a unique botanical profile, some traditional and some, like the floral BLOOM and the spiced Opihr, that embrace the current trends of adding a little extra flare. As a boss, Joanne has commented that sense of smell, over other factors such as gender, informs her team building; as an innovator, she says the "connection between science and creativity" is key.

One does not have to be a bar owner, distiller, or marketing guru to find a place in the booze business. Glendalough Distillery in Wicklow, Ireland, has long captured my imagination with its emphasis on seasonal botanical builds in its gins. Aside from the status of being one of Ireland's very first craft distilleries, it has the fascinating practice of making gins from locally foraged plants. Professional forager Geraldine Kavanagh has a lifetime of experience finding local edible plants in Wicklow. As a part of her foraging business—one that includes paid "foraging walks" around the region—she provides seasonal, local botanicals to the Glendalough Distillery. This, for me, is the ultimate expression of terroir in a spirit. Through Kavanagh's work, the distillers are able to take what sets gin apart—unique botanical flavors—and use only what can be gathered wild from the soil around the distillery. As the conversation around terroir and sustainability in the spirits world continues, roles in the industry will evolve, and new professions like Kavanagh's could emerge in exciting ways.

The Art of Being There

I knew Talia Baiocchi already, in theory. I'd been introduced to her by a mutual friend when I first had my bartending chops and was looking to spread the word on craft cocktails. *Punch*, the on-line magazine of which she is editor in chief, was a phenomenal source of information, not just for drink recipes and trends, but for how drinks intersected with culture. Big-picture stuff.

I'm not sure what made Talia take the chance on an unproven recent MFA graduate who sent her five too-long pitches, but she did. Over the course of four years I wrote my most insightful liquor stories for *Punch*, all delving into some nerdy enclave of liquor and culture. I wrote about how Irish whiskey was poised for a comeback and about how barreled gins tasted awesome. I did my best to appear professional, scatterbrained and overwhelmed with bar shifts as I was. So it was a real joy when she replied to my request for an interview.

For all the emailing, I knew little of her story. I knew she'd worked in wine retail and had been the wine editor at *Eater* before *Punch* made its debut in 2014. What I hadn't known was how young Talia had been at each of these milestones and the kind of blistering criticism she'd endured, as only the internet age can provide.

Talia Baiocchi
Photo Credit: Lizzie Munro

Speaking to her on the phone for the first time, I was not surprised by her brisk and forthright manner of speaking. Having come to know the *Punch* house "voice" (the tone in which all articles are phrased; every magazine has its own), her speech patterns were familiar. In fact, starting my booze-writing career on her site did me a favor. I learned how to cram the most information possible into each sentence. This was true of Talia's speech as well. She wasted no time. It made me miss Queens a little.

I knew that Talia was from California, had gone to school in New York City, and, after college, had left for Italy to work in vineyards. I asked her what inspired her to study wine in the first place.

"I was working as a hostess at a restaurant in the East Village, and I started learning about wine there through staff tastings, then I started reading and getting involved with industry tastings from there, but I had no idea what the 'wine world' meant. At that point it wasn't quite as rich and diverse as it is now. Sommeliers were not yet rock stars in the way they are now and all that. I was sort of like, *I'm into this.*"

Sure, she was into wine, but what was the endgame? Did she envision any particular career coming from it?

She laughed. "I really wasn't thinking about that. I was working in restaurants. I had studied journalism and political science in college. I was sort of like, *I don't see a clear career path for myself.* What I do know is that while I was working at the restaurant I fell in love with wine. I felt like I had one shot to pursue that passion and see where it took me, even though I also had no idea what kind of career opportunities existed in the wine world."

This was not the first time Talia felt called to a seemingly impractical topic. After high school, she said, she had wanted to study art history, but felt pressured to go into something more practical. Unfortunately, journalism and political science hadn't yielded opportunities she'd been excited about. "The internships I did...I worked on a [political] campaign, I hated that."

"I was like, *I'm not going to make this mistake again.* I had the same kind of connection with [wine] that I did with art history in high school."

Following this instinct, she booked a ticket to Italy, mind and return date wide open. She worked the harvest in Piedmont, and spent the rest of the summer hitting up every wine region she could until resources ran out.

"When I came back I was just like, all right, I'm just going to see what I can do with the knowledge that I've gathered over the past couple of years, and kind of took it from there. In a roundabout way, I ended up back in journalism, even though truthfully I graduated with no intention of necessarily being a writer or journalist." Haha, younger self.

"[Writing] was something I always did from a young age, it was the thing in school I was best at, but I didn't see myself, after going through college, having a career as a journalist." Particularly since her professors at NYU tried their best to put a damper on their students' ambitions. They'd say, for instance, that journalism was "not the glamorous career that it used to be, nobody has any money anymore, it's tough to break into." She'd taken these warnings to heart.

"It's interesting that it took something I really loved to find my way back to writing. I think I just needed that thing. I needed a thing I wanted to write about in order to see a path to a career."

Upon her return from Italy, Talia got a job at wine retailer Italian Wine Merchants. She ended up in a specialty sales division, selling blue-chip wines from Italy and France to high end clients. This sounds terrifying to me, but it was key to her continuing wine education.

"I cold-called people. I was twenty-two. I made some big sales and got some big clients, and got to drink a lot of amazing wine that these days is impossible to have access to without tons of money. It was a tremendous opportunity for me. I wouldn't have the basic knowledge of wine if it wasn't for that experience, that few years, being able to drink the classic wines of the world."

This reminded me of my second office job, at the Met Opera in New York. At twenty-five, I saw dozens of world-class singers, enjoyed shows I would have had no chance of affording otherwise, schmoozed with donors who gave away annually twice or more than what I made in a year. All this because I could write and (to a lesser degree) talk. For an NYU graduate such as Talia with a gift for banter, high-end wine sales made perfect sense. But this position would not hold her long.

"From there I went to launch a startup with my friend August Cardona, who was my boss at Italian Wine Merchants." They were tasked with establishing the New York arm of a UK startup that published reviews of restaurant wine lists. Talia helped populate and edit their review database. This was edgier than it might sound. Wine reviews are old news: the critic assesses an individual wine's quality, gives tasting notes, suggests pairings. Publishing assessments of a wine list was novel. Wine lists are most often put together by the restaurant's sommelier, a position far more lauded now than ten years ago thanks to a barrage of popular documentaries and books about the rigors of the Master Sommelier Examination. The wine list is a testament to the sommelier's taste and creativity, and their ability to work within (or aim above) the budgets and expectations of the restaurant's clientele. These reviews intertwined the wine and service worlds on paper as they are in real life. Food media took notice.

"I did that, launched it, and that ended up becoming a column on *Eater*. From there I became the wine editor for *Eater*."

Talia's *Eater* columns were popular; she represented a young and knowledgeable voice in the wine writing field—a relative rarity at the time. As such, her work was often met with commenter ire for her daring having-of-opinions as a young woman, and the unorthodoxy of a wine list review to begin with. Personally, I think the first two decades of the twenty-first century will go down in history as the time when the internet gave public platforms to every mean-spirited dolt with a keyboard, and we will be ashamed of it. No matter. Talia had bigger things to think about.

"I was doing a bunch of freelance writing, then I met Aaron Wehner, who is the publisher of Ten Speed Press, at a wine dinner in Napa. We hit it off and we stayed in touch. He knew I was really interested in sherry, and he sent me an email one day and he asked if I want to write a book about it. I was like, 'Sure!' I had no idea what that would necessarily entail." I could relate to this.

"The point of all of this is I kind of just said yes and jumped into things without ever really knowing exactly what they would entail. I just had faith that I could pull it off, and I think that's the one through line through all of this stuff. It wasn't like I had some master plan. I think a lot of it was luck and timing and meeting the right people, but also just jumping in and not having fear."

Wehner helped her find an agent, helped her through the process of writing and publishing *Sherry*—part a story of her travels through the region of Jerez, visiting *bodegas* (wineries) and learning about sherry's production; part tasting guide complete with cocktail recipes. It took about a year and a half to complete.

"Sherry is incredibly complex and in many ways unknowable. Also in many ways [Jerez is] a rich and paradoxical place. I only skimmed the surface of that. I attempted to write the book in a way that brought the reader along with that journey, not as somebody writing as some kind of expert on high. I was genuinely learning at the same time."

At the same time her first book was launching, Talia's mentor had another question: Would she be interested in starting a website about wine and spirits that spoke to her demographic?

"At that point, I had barely edited anything, and I was like just a freelance writer that had made a name for myself in New York within our very small world. I said, 'Sure!'" At this she laughed, as if she could hardly believe it herself. "Then over the course of the next eight months [we came] up with the idea of *Punch*, and I brought on Leslie Pariseau, who was a good friend of mine, as deputy editor." Leslie came from the spirits side of the business, while Talia came from wine. "We both have a similar writing style and aesthetic and all that. We clicked creatively. Together we launched the site and grew it from there." The two went on to cowrite another book, *Spritz*, about Italian *aperitivo* cocktails.

Punchdrink.com launched in 2014. It focused on the intersection of drinks and culture, with an emphasis on long-form narrative journalism. That is, seeing beer, wine, and spirits as "a means to discover the sense of

66

I kind of just said yes
and jumped into things
without ever really knowing
exactly what they would
entail. I just had faith that
I could pull it off.

99

" A lot of people ask me about being a woman, and it wasn't so much about being a woman but more about being young. Wine hasn't been particularly hospitable to young voices until recently. That's another piece of advice: just be honest about what you know and don't know. "

'place' psychologically ingrained into a region over centuries—or a peek into a specific era and its ambitions." It's all terroir all the time.

I had heard previous interviews with her in which she mentioned what she felt was rampant discrimination against younger writers in the wine world. I asked her how she approached the experiences of being the editor in chief of a major drinks site and publishing her first booze book at this time, knowing there could be pushback.

"I always tried to be honest about whether I did or did not know something. It's an uncomfortable place to be, being young, in my mid- to late twenties. I was twenty-eight when *Punch* launched and I felt really insecure about that. Sometimes, especially with *Eater*, people would kind of come after me and put me down, because I think there was definitely ageism there. A lot of people ask me about being a woman, and it wasn't so much about being a woman but more about being young. Wine hasn't been particularly hospitable to young voices until recently. That's another piece of advice: just be honest about what you know and don't know. Which is hard for a lot of people."

In 2015 *Punch* won a Tales of the Cocktail Spirited Award for Best Cocktail & Spirits Publication. It became a source for information about obscure liqueurs, affordable and unusual wine recommendations, cocktail recipes, and stories about a city's drinking culture. It was a rare middle ground between a general-interest magazine and a trade publication in that it appealed to people inside the industry and out. It started, and remains, digital only. I asked Talia if she had any print ambitions for it.

"*Punch*, from the very beginning, [has been] a digital magazine that's essentially part of the gigantic publisher—not just Ten Speed but Penguin Random House. There's always been a real interest in trying to bring these tools together and have a brand that can be in both [digital and print] spaces in a meaningful way. I think we do that in the books." Starting this year, Ten Speed Press will publish books under the *Punch* brand. Still, "Digital is always going to be our priority and where we live; we are going to explore that relationship and how we can be in print in different ways." She said they are exploring a print magazine extension of the brand, "not

If you want to be a part of this industry, be a part of this industry. Be curious and ask questions and be open. It's cliché, it's assumed knowledge, but I don't think that a lot of people realize how important that simple thing is.

a monthly or even a quarterly, maybe just a biyearly. A place where we can really flex our muscles a little bit and do some of those really big stories that deserve the kind of epic treatment that print can offer, that sometimes feels impermanent on the web."

She thought for a moment, and continued: "Every time we see a lot of photography that ends up on the cutting-room floor, and a lot of stuff that feels like it would be more dynamic visually if we were able to lay it out in print. It's not only about the text but about the visuals, and that's an especially important part of who we are." Beautiful photography has always been central to *Punch*'s identity. A print magazine ensures that photos are viewed in their best formats, rather than someone's cracked smart phone screen. Rather than prioritizing one medium over another from an abstract notion of worth, why not choose based on content?

It seemed that Talia's publishing career, which she had given up and then come back around to via wine and spirits, was still growing. There was one more thing weighing on me. Talia had mentioned earlier that she established her writing career at a time "when it was possible to do so." I asked her what she meant by that.

It's not that people can't make a living by writing about wine and spirits, she says, "it's two things. There's a lot more people who are in it. I think there's a lot more competition, but there's also a lot more opportunity. I don't know how that compares if you look at the balance today vs. the balance five years ago. I feel like there was a moment where it was quite easy to have more access."

Access to what, exactly? People. Building relationships in the writing world is important, she said, and as the scene becomes more crowded, that part becomes more challenging.

"I don't mean this in a superficial way. You hear people say, 'Oh, you need to go out and build relationships,' and [it] feels like something where you have an agenda and it feels disingenuous. It's more like if you want to be a part of this industry, be a part of this industry. Be curious and ask questions and be open. It's cliché, it's assumed knowledge, but I don't think that a lot of people realize how important that simple thing is."

Being honest about what you know and being open, interested, and nice to people. These were her two big pieces of advice for those coming up in the booze-writing world. I could handle that.

Part Three:
Shaking It

9

Modern Matriarchs

The modern cocktail scene has long been defined by nostalgia, usually for times well before most of us were born. Cocktail writers tend to speak on certain eras of drinking as the "bad old days" or the "dark age of cocktails," indicating the years roughly between the late 1960s and the turn of the twenty-first century. These were much improved times, I should point out, for things like civil rights for people of color, opportunities for women, LGBTQ acceptance, and other great ideas. Cocktails, though, not so much.

There are plenty of books written on this subject. The cocktail—that uniquely American invention from the nineteenth century that defined drinking fashions until Prohibition—has died and been reborn at least once. Pinpointing the exact reason for the cocktail's decline from a fresh, vibrant fixture of gastronomy to the syrupy-sweet, artificially colored and flavored drinks found in nightclubs is like trying to give one single cause for World War I. Baby boomers' distaste for their parents' alcoholic interests, club culture, singles' bars, the rise of processed foods—all these things bear a bit of the blame. Even the somewhat reviled term "mixologist" is nothing new; saloon owner and bartender Jerry Thomas called himself this, as did countless bar impresarios of the 1800s cocktail heyday. What has become pretentious was invented in a spirit of fun.

When the classic cocktail revival / craft cocktail resurgence / whatever you want to call it began in New York in the early 2000s, it was undeniably a turning point in drink history. Dale DeGroff is frequently written about as a kind of ur-progenitor, and he was certainly instrumental in spreading the word. One of the most important and exciting aspects of this scene, for me, was how women were bosses from the beginning. Audrey Saunders and Julie Reiner are the unquestioned matriarchs of the modern cocktail scene. Their bars—Pegu Club, Clover Club, Flatiron Lounge, to mention a few—are long-standing institutions in a city where restaurants turn over by the hour, and the list of bartenders they have trained reads like the cast of a "history of modern bars" movie. Charlotte Voisey brought style, speed, and panache from the UK and showed everyone what exactly a brand ambassador looked like. While this did not mean the bar world turned into a gender utopia (now *that's* far from the truth), the founding members of this club being prominent and respected women set a more progressive starting point.

Protégés of Audrey Saunders include PDT founder Jim Meehan, Death & Co.'s Phil Ward and Brian Miller, and consultants Chad Solomon and Toby Maloney, making her the mixological root of the most influential bar programs in the country. Julie Reiner's Clover Club fostered Lynnette Marrero and Ivy Mix, who would go on to found Speed Rack, the ultimate national bartending competition for women, and renowned bartenders franky marshall and Jillian Vose, both alumni of the Dead Rabbit bar, to name a few. Read an interview with any of these bartenders and the theme is common: as mentors, Saunders and Reiner set them up for greatness.

I don't want to rewrite any of the fine books and films on the New York school of cocktails, but I do have a few favorite New York bartenders— ones I tried and tried and failed to connect with. I left NYC in 2013 after a ten-year stay that included twelve different apartments. As a New York expat, people certainly love to ask me if I miss it. I still can't answer this, not because it's complicated, but because the question makes no sense.

ms. franky marshall
Photo Credit: Jason Rowan

The city is not a singular entity; it's a big messed-up morass of human dwellings, in which live many people and lots of food that I love. I had my first nice drink in Williamsburg at the Hotel Delmano and blindly stumbled into some of the world's best bars by accident over the years. But when I briefly considered moving back to open a bar with my first mentor a few years ago, I realized most of my memories of the place involved being broke and depressed. So I stayed out west, in the Golden State, where there is a fine number of world-famous bars and plenty of vitamin D. Which is why, if I'm being superstitious, I think the city went out of its way to stop me from meeting franky marshall. Because NYC is a spiteful old broad, and I would've *loved* that.

After a brief encounter at Tales of the Cocktail, when she was being inducted into the Dame Hall of Fame in 2017, I was supposed to meet ms. franky, as she is known, at her Brooklyn Heights cocktail lounge, Le Boudoir. Nature was against me, though. There was an impenetrable blizzard, and I still kick myself for not visiting in September like a sane person.

ms. franky is a fast-rising icon and a perfect example of this decade's high profile bartenders. She is a polyglot and trained musician with the passport stamps and personal style of a rock star, and a woman of color in a still very monochrome industry. She can typically be seen with shades of purple in her hair, makeup, and/or outfit and seems to blend vintage style with a rock-'n'-roll sensibility. When accepting her Dame Hall of Fame honor, she practically chasséd up to the podium dressed in a 1950s-style purple sweater and skirt set and a complementary head scarf, like a grown-up, punk rock Natalie Wood.

"Hello, dahlings," she purred.

For all the charms and trappings of her persona, when ms. franky started to speak, her training and knowledge was evident. Her acceptance speech was all about those who helped her along the way and to whom she hoped to pay it forward. She acknowledged there are "always times

Keep your minds open to
every experience. I take
everything in, and I find
inspiration everywhere.

when we need a little bit of help. It's very important for us to continue that mentorship." She had no problem asking for help, she said, and was now in the nice position of having "baby bartenders" come ask her for mentorship. She would be an excellent resource.

During a panel discussion she led in 2016 at Invasion Cocktail in Montreal, ms. franky recounted starting her hospitality career as a server, eventually "lying [her] way behind the bar" since the bartenders seemed to be having more fun and making more money. "It was easy then," she recalled, working at a non-cocktail bar. Vodka, soda, sour mix, shots. Boom. It was difficult to be in the bar scene in New York at that time, though, and not be exposed to this "craft cocktail" thing. It was not long before she started to educate herself about spirits and cocktails and began applying for more difficult bar jobs. After a string of getting nonresponses to her applications, she was hired by Julie Reiner to be a server at the Clover Club in 2008, which started an educational journey that took her through the Tales of the Cocktail Apprentice Program (three times!), training through BarSmarts and the Wine & Spirits Education Trust, and a weeklong stage (pronounced *stah-j*) at 69 Colebrooke Row in London. During all this training, she tended bar at such high-caliber cocktail joints as the Clover Club, the Dead Rabbit, and the Holiday Cocktail Lounge (which, to my surprise, evolved from the dive I knew it as in my NYC years). She does category work promoting French spirits and travels the world in search of new culinary delights. In 2016 she became the beverage director of the French rococo, Marie Antoinette–inspired Le Boudoir in Brooklyn and continues to give educational presentations on the cocktail circuit all over the world.

The key is soaking up every bit of information on your passion and asking for help to get what you want. When asked at the Dame Hall of Fame ceremony what advice she would give to young people and to her fifteen-year-old self, ms. franky replied, "Keep your minds open to every experience. I take everything in, and I find inspiration everywhere." To her fifteen-year-old self she would tell her that pink is a better color than orange for her hair.

There is a bar called Big Bar in my neighborhood in Los Angeles, and its boss is a big boss. Figuratively speaking. The bar is about 150 square feet, one-half of a converted bungalow. The boss is Cari Hah. It's the kind of place that makes me happy I live here, even when other things are making me unhappy. It's low-key and neighborhood-y, but the cocktails are on point, and the bartenders are unafraid to go off-menu.

Everyone knows Cari. She has the kind of online presence that makes the envious roll their eyes—personal and enthusiastic. As Cari demonstrates, the Facebook/Instagram publicity model sets the stage to upset old orders and monolithic power structures. It allows for infiltration of old boys' clubs. It beckons the thirsty.

When we sat down on the Big Bar patio, Cari had an overstuffed clipboard under her arm and a huge water bottle with lemons and mint floating in it. I'd already hit the bar for my go-to day drink, a Cocchi Americano and soda, and made small talk with the bartender, Mario, while she finished up her business. When we sat down, I told her about how I wanted to interview all the badass women I'd met working in this business and publish the stories about the hardships they faced as women in the industry. She responded with some caution.

"People who have written articles about [this]," she began, "their question is always about 'What are the challenges that you face as a woman in the industry?' Which is fine, obviously there are challenges, but for me the bigger thing was being an Asian in the industry," she went on. "For me, the race thing was even more than being a woman thing. Because there's a lot of women in the industry. [There are] bars that only want women for their looks—that was never my role, because I look the way I look, I don't have that sort of body...and I don't play that card anyway."

Cari began bartending seriously in 2009, right when the craft cocktail movement was starting to take off in LA. She had tended bar in a club in college, before moving on to a career in investment banking, which she hated. She walked away from her job at Goldman Sachs and eventually found her calling behind the bar.

Cari Hah
Photo Credit: @eugeneshoots

"[Craft cocktailing] was kind of still a frontier," Cari said, "so I just kind of fell into that style of bartending instead of club bartending. And I was like, *This is totally different...actually learning about the liquor.*"

Aha, I thought. *The nerd trap. I know it well.*

"I've always loved alcohol, not just to get drunk but because I love the flavor of the spirits, the process of making it, distillation and history and all that was so fascinating to me. Even when I was in finance, I made money without having time to spend it so I would just buy bottles of really expensive or interesting liquor because I thought it was amazing, not really knowing anything about what I was buying, but thinking if it was expensive it must be good. I learned a lot though in trying all those different bottles. I love to study, I like knowing things. So learning about all the different liquors was a whole new world for me."

Cari was the first, but far from the last, bartender to confirm my suspicion that we are secret academics at heart. It is 100 percent noncoincidental that I threw myself so hard into learning about bars and spirits immediately after I left my graduate writing program. I had been so used to reading, asking questions, creating things. The vacuum left after my thesis was printed was painful, but I was terrified to write anything new after years of workshop feedback. So I found a new outlet and went bananas—cocktail books, extra shifts, coming in on off-days for research and development. This pattern would become familiar, the more bartenders I spoke with.

I asked Cari where she got her start making cocktails in her second career.

"I opened Izakaya Fu-Ga, in Japantown, and I did cocktails for the bar and I was the bartender there, then I also started working at a jazz club, also in J-Town, called the Blue Whale, which is an amazing jazz club. Then I was working the door at the Varnish and learning from all the bartenders like Eric [Alperin] at the Varnish in the very early days."

The Varnish is one of the bars that helped finally establish Los Angeles as a place to get a great cocktail, and it was only the beginning. I moved here in 2014, after bartenders like Julian Cox and Aidan Demarest had seeded the town with great cocktail programs, and you could find a place to serve you an old-fashioned on a giant ice cube in pretty much any neighborhood. I asked her what the atmosphere was like when the cocktail scene was shiny and new.

"It was definitely the new and exciting thing. It was so new, those kinds of cocktails with the ice that nobody'd ever seen...and there was a lot of cache there. [At the Varnish] we had a really strict door policy back then, and it's a small space so there was always a line."

I was learning through the course of our conversation that Cari seemed to love a challenge. Her next move was to help open a cocktail bar with Aidan Demarest called Neat, in Glendale. "We were trying to bring a better sort of cocktail to the area. We broke ground up there, and it was tough." Glendale is a semi-suburban independent city nestled next to Los Angeles and more generally known for its shopping malls.

"The neighborhood wasn't understanding [at first] what we were trying to do, and then they started to get a hold of it, so we did very well there, but it was always run on a shoestring budget. I learned a lot about managing there. I can probably manage a bar off of zero money because I did it there."

Go ahead and turn that struggle into a positive, I thought. At this point, it was clear that her "temporary" foray into bartending was evolving into something much bigger.

"In the meantime, Facebook was becoming a platform on which you could promote yourself. Me and my best friend, Jaymee Mandeville, who was running the bar Drago [Centro] at the time, kind of connected over our love of agave [spirits] and creating these sangritas to go with agave. So we started pimping ourselves out as guest bartenders, with sponsorship from different brands to do guest nights and create a whole menu of sangritas." Sangrita is a nonalcoholic drink that originated in Mexico, typically a blend of fruit and vegetable juice with some spice element, served alongside high-end tequila as a palate cleanser.

"We did it at almost every major bar at the time just for fun. Just because we loved it." She would use Facebook to promote her events, spreading the word and growing a community at the same time. "At Neat I learned a lot about production and about throwing events, because no one throws an event like Aidan Demarest. No one throws a party like that man does."

Working under different managers, picking up new skills at different gigs, she built her toolbox. "All these little roles got me all the experience that you need in the liquor industry if you want to make a name for yourself."

This is what fundamentally distinguishes today's cocktail scene from what I knew as bartending growing up. The figures of Coach and Woody from *Cheers*, for example, were not intended to be role models for culinary talents. These were good people, but lunkheads whom nobody felt bad telling their problems to, because at the end of the day, it could be worse. You could *be* them.

Cari embodies the twenty-first-century bartender—sharp, ambitious, and educated. Not necessarily college educated, though many are that, but definitely well versed in the history and technique of their craft. You *can* make a name for yourself, because the community extends beyond the neighborhood. The cocktail community is international, and there are adventures to be had (not to mention money to be made) by getting involved. Aside from working at bars and doing her own events, how did she gain experience and make cocktail friends?

"I went to Camp Runamok. Lush Life Productions does a lot of booze events, and the first year they decided to do Camp Runamok; it's a bourbon [summer] camp, basically. It's in Kentucky, and you have to apply, and if you get accepted then you get to go to these bourbon distilleries and meet all these other bartenders from all over the US. I was in that first group that went and I got to meet a bunch of my contacts." As you might imagine, those who were in that first group have also gone on to do interesting things in the industry. I mentioned how I used to have reservations about professional networking, that it all seemed a bit phony, but have since realized that if I meet people who do the same work as I do, and like it as much as I do, why would I *not* befriend them?

"Exactly. So we kind of came up together, knowing that this is our career and we want to be somebody in this career, but we were still working on it. So now I have this network of people I can reach out to all the time, and I'll read about my friends in the news, and it's so fun...it was just this sort of organic thing."

Another "organic" thing happened her first night bartending at Neat. There was a man at the bar who seemed to be friends with the boss. "It was my very first shift and I was a little nervous because it was just me—I was the only bartender, there were no barbacks, and Aidan's no help. So he decides it would be fun to order a round of Ramos Gin Fizzes for the whole bar. Every single person in there." If you've never had a Ramos Gin Fizz, it's a bucket-list drink—ethereal in design and flavor. But make sure you go someplace that advertises them, or that you're married to the bartender, because the Ramos is an infamously difficult drink that, when made in the traditional way, takes up to fifteen minutes to make and stands in for a biceps workout. The lore goes that in nineteenth-century New Orleans, bartenders would line up a dozen low-paid laborers to shake the drinks for Mardi Gras crowds.

"I thought he was joking when he told me to do it, but he was like, 'No, I'm serious, get to it.' So I was like, 'Eekay . . .' and I just did it. My new boss just told me to do this so I just did it. The gentleman who was sitting at the bar was watching me the whole night. Toward the end of the night—we'd been chatting but I didn't really know who he was—he says, 'Have you heard of Tales of the Cocktail?' and I was like, 'Not really. I know it's the place where all the important bartenders in LA go every summer, but I don't really know what it is.' He said, 'My name is Paul Tuennerman, I'm one of the founders of Tales of the Cocktail and I've been watching you work. You need to apply to the apprenticeship program.'"

After applying and being accepted into the Cocktail Apprentice Program at Tales, Cari joined another set of bar world alumni.

"Basically the apprentices do all the cocktails for the whole week. For all the seminars, all the events, the apprentices are the backstage production of the whole [festival]. So from that experience, I learned all about batching and event production for the big-style events for five hundred to one thousand to ten thousand people. It was incredibly helpful for me at the time, because now I have event production...I have bartending experience, cocktailing experience, I even know how to run a door and I know how to run a floor, I know how to social media promote. All this while I'm just studying. Studying liquor, studying things."

What was next? She seemed hell-bent on tackling every aspect of the industry. Oh, right: brand work.

"I fell in love with cachaça and I was approached by Leblon." Cachaça (pronounced *cah-SHA-suh*) is a Brazilian spirit made from pressed sugarcane juice, similar to but not the same as rum. Cari set out to spread the word.

"[Leblon Cachaça] had heard of this random Asian girl who was a bartender in LA that was talking all about cachaça and doing cocktails with it and who knew how to use it. They were like, 'Amazing, who is this girl? We need to talk to her.' So they hired me to be a part-time ambassador. They didn't call it that at the time but that's what it was. My nickname was Ninja de Cachaça."

She began the brand ambassador life, doing trainings, going to bars and talking about the spirit, traveling to Brazil to the corporate office, and making cocktails for use in marketing materials. She also did part-time brand work for Suntory.

"I loved doing part-time everything, because I could make my schedule the way I wanted. That's always been my attitude: I don't need this job, but I want this job because I would take on any opportunity to learn something new. That's my approach to everything. In the liquor business you can literally make your own path. I grew up in an Asian household—my whole family is doctors. It's a very set path. You go to a good college, you go to a good med school, then you do a good residency, then you do this and you do this and boom, you're a doctor. So I even took the path less traveled by going into finance because I didn't want to be a doctor. But then I said, 'This is misery, this is ridiculous, I'm not doing this.' I made it to associate level but then I was like, 'Fuck this. I'm out.'"

217

"

I loved doing part-time everything, because I could make my schedule the way I wanted. That's always been my attitude: I don't need this job, but I would take on any opportunity to learn something new. That's my approach to everything. In the liquor business you can make your own path.

"

When she put it this way, it occurred to me that once you've upset your family with your life choices and still become successful, there's little left to be afraid of. It is the ideal state for a person to find their own way.

"In liquor, there's no set path. It's not like you have to be a barback and then a bartender and then a manager. I decided early on that I wanted to be good at bartending; I wanted to learn about liquor; I wanted to do events. I did everything I wanted, because I just put my mind to it and was like, *Yes, this is what we are going to do.* Whether you're a girl or not, in this business you can carve your own path and that's really exciting."

It may be true that there is no set path to bartending greatness, but Cari did acknowledge some roadblocks to diversity when so much of the profession's skills are handed down from mentor to mentee in the bar.

"It is a boys' club in a way. Especially in LA, where you have the families of bars…the big bar groups. Where if you don't come up in this family or this family you wonder…how are you going to get hired? For me, I was not in a family. I just did it my own way."

The "families" Cari referred to are the handful of bar groups and consultancies that had so far been responsible for a disproportionate number of important bar openings in the city. This model makes sense: elaborate bar programs take a lot of capital to open, and it helps to have the backing of a large organization or have a high-profile bartender designing your menus and training your staff. It has led to a certain amount of homogenization of the cocktail scene, for better or for worse. Hearing from someone who was largely self-educated was a welcome change. As consumers, we might have to trust our palates rather than looking to the bar's lineage to know what's good. As for the celebrity bartender, Cari had thoughts on this.

"The bar is a stage, but you are not the star. Your guest is the star. I felt like, for a while, it had gotten flipped, where the bartender was like, *I am famous,* or *I want to be famous, look at me.*" This was an interesting turn, considering her experience with self-promotion via Facebook and guest-bartending gigs. But she made it clear that there is no place for ego behind the bar. "In my bar family," that is, her Big Bar "family" whose creations,

The bar is a stage, but you are not the star. Your guest is the star. I felt like, for a while, it had gotten flipped, where the bartender was like, I am famous, or I want to be famous, look at me.

shenanigans, and events she exuberantly touts on her social media feed, "it should not matter who is behind the bar, your drink should always taste the same, and you should always feel welcome, and you should always get great service."

I met Mary Bartlett in the Upstairs Bar, on the roof of the Ace Hotel in downtown Los Angeles. Mary was introduced to me as the beverage director of the hotel. This perplexed me, since I knew the Ace had at least three drinking venues, one of which was a large event space. Did one person manage all that? I would find out soon enough.

Mary was running late. She had been talking to the LA Fire Department about the alarms going off because of some production hiccup at the theater. It was fine, I said, refraining from making a dad joke about yelling "Fire!" in a theater. She was small and newly dark-haired, clad in all black with low-heeled boots.

Mary came to LA five years ago from Portland, Oregon without a job lined up. She'd spent her whole adult life in Portland, most of it working in hospitality. For reasons that will become clear, she came south ready and determined to build a great career.

A few days after she landed in Los Angeles, Mary met with Dave Kaplan, Alex Day, and Devon Tarby of Proprietors LLC, the group behind Death & Co. and the Walker Inn, et al. She had heard they were opening a new bar. That bar would be called Honeycut, and Mary was part of the opening crew.

Honeycut was a big deal in Los Angeles's cocktail scene when it opened in 2013. It was among the first places in town to combine quality cocktails with a kitschy, themed dance venue. It represented a step away from the ultra-serious cocktail den that dominated the scene in its infancy, offering tasty drinks with some dumb fun thrown in. Mary found her groove there quickly.

"Once we were a month in I got promoted [to manager]. When our GM left a few months later I became the assistant general manager. I stayed there for three years and also did a lot of consulting work with Proprietors, helped open other bars." She also worked part-time with as a brand ambassador for Grey Goose vodka and other brands, developing recipes and training bartenders on how to use their products.

It was hard to keep up as she listed off her responsibilities with Proprietors. I could imagine it was much more hectic to live it.

"It was a lot of fun" she said, responding to my raised eyebrows, "I learned so much."

While bar work can be an incredible teacher of skills, technical knowledge, and insight, it can also be a ravenous, time-sucking beast. For those of us inclined to say yes to all opportunities (or have boundary issues), it can devour days and weeks with no regard for birthdays, holidays, weddings, or funerals.

"I worked all the time. I would take maybe one day off a week." These were hardly your standard eight-hour workdays. "I would get up in the morning and go do Proprietors brand stuff, then I would go to Honeycut and do admin, and then I would work [bartending] shifts and close the bar."

"Close the bar" means not just staying until 2:00 or 3:00 in the morning (later in other states), but having to clean, count, and restock the whole bar. It is tedious and physical work for tired bodies and brains, and it requires a special level of care to be consistent.

"Even when I cut back on shifts, I was still closing the bar Tuesday, Thursday, Friday, and Saturday. I just worked all the time. I had a bit of a crisis in my body and brain. I couldn't even sleep, I was so full of anxiety." She started to wonder: "What am I doing it for?"

For most bartenders, reaching this point signals an exit from the industry. The time and physical commitments can grind you down, and burnout looms. In a tipped profession, there are rarely incremental pay raises, and no accrual of things like medical benefits, retirement plans, or paid time off for the majority of us. It's simply not part of the business model in bars and restaurants that operate on slim profit margins even under the best conditions.

"I realized I didn't want to close the bar anymore, that I wanted to figure out what it was to have a life. I'd been in the service industry since I was nineteen," said the thirty-year-old Mary.

"I had a moment when one of my friends from college wanted me to be in her wedding. She's like, 'I totally get that you might not be able to... and you might not be able to make it to the wedding.' Just the way that she gave me the out already, I realized: *I don't go to anything for anyone I love, unless they're also in the service industry.*"

This hit close to home. I recalled sighingly taking time off for family events and thinking about all the money I was losing, being there and not working. The immediate cash of a bartending gig is addictive, and like any addictive substance, can warp one's perspective. Mary wanted to stay in the field she loved, but was determined to get out of the night shift grind.

"It took me about three months of constantly talking with people and interviewing," before she found what she wanted. The Ace Hotel was across the street from Honeycut and she would often visit when she felt like escaping her bar's subterranean dance den. The beverage director at the time would tell her when jobs were opening up.

"My response was always 'Tell me when your job is available, because that's the job I want.' Eventually, he called. I'd always wanted to work in hotels because in a lot of ways I think it's the ultimate form of hospitality. You get to fully take care of someone. We have a lot of locals, but also we get to host people in our city and be like, 'This is LA. LA's not scary, LA is wonderful!'"

For the next two years, Mary was the beverage director for the entire Ace Hotel property. She managed everything alcohol related for the Upstairs Bar on the roof, a couple of event spaces on the hotel's second floor, the ground-floor restaurant, and the 1,600-seat Theatre at the Ace Hotel, which includes beer, wine, and spirits in its concessions sales.

What does it mean to "oversee the beverages"? A few things. Deciding what goes on the drinks menus, for one. Also, a whole lot of counting.

"Inventory is a monster here," she said, when I asked what the tougher parts of the job were. For those (un)fortunate enough never to have inventoried a bar, in even the smallest venue it's a tedious process. If a bar wants to track spending and prevent theft, the management is tasked with counting the bottles on the shelves and in storage, typically every one to two weeks. My last gig had more than three hundred different brands of liquor, plus beer and wine, plus however many backup bottles were in the storeroom. That was just one bar; Mary had four and a theater.

"It's a terrible, terrible long day. What it means for me is that I come in early, before anyone has to touch the spaces." Some of her team helps, but in the end, "I count a bunch of different areas for hours, then I input every part of a bottle of anything in an Excel sheet." She and the team were constantly working on improving the system. Personally, I thought this would be a great job for robots.

The upside of being accountable for all those bottles, however, was being in charge of purchasing—deciding what each venue was going to sell. At first, this meant educating herself on her "weak spots," like wine. She recalled her surprise when she learned the restaurants didn't employ a sommelier to build their wine lists.

"I said, 'I know I buy things, but who picks things?' and they were like, 'That's you!'" She was daunted at first, but took it as an opportunity: "That's actually one of the coolest parts of my job. I'd always wanted to learn about wine, and I finally just had to. I dove right in."

She emphasized the need to self-educate, hard. Even beyond the potential embarrassment of a wine list faux pas in a venue where locals and visitors converge in large numbers year-round, she thought of the long game.

"If I do a bad job, everyone I know and anyone I'll want to work with in the future, or the people I need to invest or believe in me, are all going to see my work, so I better get good at things really fast."

Apparently, she did get good at things, with a combination of study and trusting her colleagues.

"When you have that many decisions to make, you have to surround yourself with people that are informed and want to help you make those decisions. You can't be inspired about everything and you can't be the most informed about everything." She gave this example: "I would say the category I knew the least about was beer. I'd been a beer purchaser for places before, but it definitely helped that I had Angela, who manages up here [on the rooftop, and] Soraya, who manages both spaces, who are both beer nerds. So I'm like: What have you been wanting to do? We share the burdens and the fun stuff."

Her job also includes managing programming for the bars, overseeing the front-of-house staff, as well as "education, hiring, training, promoting."

She took a breath. "I think that's what I do." This made me laugh. In addition to all these things, the job included a whole lot of accounting. A key responsibility of any manager is "making sure [their] numbers add up," as Mary put it. Which is tough, as the business is unpredictable and the profit margins are tight. One thing I was dying to ask about was how the hotel's wage scale affected her job. Thanks to a Los Angeles city ordinance passed a few years earlier, all hotel employees in LA earned a minimum of $15.66 an hour, before tips. That was crazy good for a tipped employee. Did this make her life harder, as the one trying to balance labor costs against sales?

"I love it," she said. "I love getting to employ people…knowing they can live their lives." The smallest smile appeared on her face: "And they get insurance and PTO." PTO. Paid time off. It's basically unheard of in this industry where the overwhelming majority of workers work fewer than forty hours a week. My entire postgraduate life was defined not only by spotty attendance at my friends' life events, but the knowledge that when I could go, I was taking a financial hit. I told her that I thought this should be the future of the industry. Then she burst my bubble.

"The model is totally flawed, though. Even with the hotel attached, once you see what's going on, it's like wow, things are tight. We're doing very well, but we still have to look at every tiny little expense just to make sure that we can afford to employ everyone."

While I dealt with my disappointment, it hit me that every manager she'd mentioned had a feminine-sounding name. Was this an all-woman management team? At this, Mary smiled wide.

"Oh my god, it's the best. I didn't know how cool it was going to be, because I've always worked for men, and in my previous few jobs I've loved it, so I didn't know anything different."

Sure, I said, there are some great male bosses, too.

"No, but the greatest male bosses are not as good as female bosses. They're so much better."

I was cracking up. I'd just hit the lady-boss mother lode. She continued. "That's what I read in these studies, and I was reading some Sheryl Sandberg stuff and she talked about role models. Then there was some study that talked about Fortune 500 companies. In all their studies, both men and women who've never had a female boss prefer a male boss. And both men and women who've had a female boss prefer a female boss. It was something where I was like, *Of course.*"

She gave an example of the kinds of differences she noticed when she came on at the Ace, a.k.a. restaurant gender utopia.

"I have Autumn, then our restaurant manager is Natasha, upstairs is Angela. For the first year I worked here the F&B manager was a woman. I remember the first preinventory meeting when I started…" The team talked about what had to be done that day, "Then they said, 'All right, does anyone have anything they need help with? Does anyone want to try something different? Does everyone feel good about what they're doing?' It was everyone working on how to help each other and do everything better. I was like, *Whoa! Women! Wow!*"

I wondered if she thought this was due to the way we are socialized.

"I think that in work we [women] accommodate the people around us and find our roles in support. When we're ambitious, wherever there's an opening, we get really good at that. We're all used to accommodating… and we're taught that we're supposed to make other people happy. Which also, in this industry, makes us good at hospitality." Imagine that. In every self-esteem/corporate-speak/self-help-guru book I've read about gender, women are chastised for feeling like they must make everyone else happy. I had never thought about it as a positive in a profession where making people happy is, well, your job.

When we're ambitious, wherever there's an opening we get really good at that. We're all used to accommodating...and we're taught that we're supposed to make other people happy. Which also, in this industry, makes us good at hospitality.

"But in the collegial sense," Mary continued as my mind exploded, "as long as we all do that stuff it's great, because no one is taking advantage of anyone."

It was difficult to know where to take the conversation from there. I had stumbled upon the world's best workplace, and the secret was putting ladies in charge. Obviously, this is not a singular cause-and-effect phenomenon, and there are some world-class horrible, terrible women bosses out there. Mary clearly liked her job and that informed her point of view. It was tremendously heartening, above all, to hear that a collaborative, communicative management force ran a moneymaking enterprise, paid people well, and looked cool doing it.

I decided to get back to Mary's roots. She'd mentioned she came from Portland: Where did she get her start in the industry?

"I started in coffee shops, which I think is the normal pre-bar thing." Correct. "Then I got a job at a cocktail bar in Portland as a server, and while I was serving there, somebody else hired me to bartend. At my original place it was really hard to get behind the bar, and [the bar owner] basically hired men and, every few years, maybe a woman. At the time, I didn't see it as the extreme problem that I see it as now, because I was young. He put me through hell to get behind the bar. I had to prove that I could do ten push-ups, which no man had to do. I had to take a shift where I had to stock all the liquor that came in, and our liquor room was...this attic cubby. You had to take an extension ladder down, extend it, climb up the ladder, and carry cases of beer up. I was a girl in my early twenties, and not that I'm small, but I definitely didn't have the strength to do that safely at all. None of the men had to take that shift every week when they worked that position. It was definitely like a prove-that-you-can-do-it thing. Now that I'm older, I totally resent him for making me do that."

I asked her if they still kept in touch. She said yes, they were cool. She's probably a better woman than I. I put forth my theory that 2008–10 was an industry-wide shift toward progress in sprits, beer, and wine. Did she notice anything like that in the bars where she worked?

She puzzled it over a moment.

When I got to LA it felt
different. It was like:
*Oh my god, I don't have
to be the girl version of my
job, I can just do my job?*

"That was ten years ago. I still think Portland is all guys. All the prominent people there are men; all the women who start to do well move away. At least in our bar scene, when I was coming up and doing well, I was like, 'Cool, there's nothing else here for me to do,' and I came here [to Los Angeles]. My close friend Lacy Hawkins moved to New York. Seriously, the men [in Portland] treated her like she was a joke. She moved to New York and she does so well: she won all these competitions [including Speed Rack in 2016], she had all these great jobs, she was at NoMad and Clover Club. She's amazing. And they were like, 'Who are you? You're nobody.' Same with like Beckaly Franks, who was at Clyde Common for a long time. She was amazing. She had to move to Hong Kong to get an opportunity."

"Recently, men in Portland have been able to talk to me about it, whereas before it would just make them uncomfortable and they'd be like, 'I don't want to get into anyone's business.' I'm like, 'You guys are living in the past.' When I got to LA it felt different. It was like: *Oh my god, I don't have to be the girl version of my job, I can just do my job? There are women doing things here?*" Women like Devon Tarby at the Varnish, Yael Vengroff at the Spare Room, and Serena Herrick and Jill Webster of Harvard and Stone. "And they didn't have to be 'one of the guys,' they could just be themselves."

The "one of the guys" trap is the worst, feeling as if you can't gain the respect of your colleagues unless you can hang, which may or may not include such activities as "taking a joke" about your sexual history, going to strip clubs, tolerating various levels of harassment, et al. . . .

"[As] I've gotten older I'm like: *No. I don't care, I'm not fun.* I care about other things so much more. I don't give a shit that you guys think I'm humorless. I'll find humor again when reps that come in stop shaking everyone else's hand and then giving me a hug."

A few months after our conversation, Mary left the Ace to pursue other projects. One can only assume they will be epic.

Misty Kalkofen's official title at Del Maguey Single Village Mezcal is *madrina*, Spanish for "godmother." This might be wry, but it is appropriate,

Misty Kalkofen
Photo credit: Maureen Ford

not only for the brand she's boosted for years but for the Boston cocktail community at large. Misty was part of the inaugural class of Dames inducted into the Tales of the Cocktail Dame Hall of Fame in 2012, and she had already been nominated years earlier for American Bartender of the Year at the Tales of the Cocktail Spirited Awards. Her accolades are numerous; in her roughly two decades of bartending she has set the bar (ahem) for knowledgeability and giving back to her community. A few of her latest endeavors, the Toast Club and the Sisterhood Project, help women directly through philanthropy and education. In the words of her friend Kirsten Amann, another Boston-based bartender, "Misty is the real deal."

Misty's storied career is further confirmation that when Jerry Thomas dubbed himself the "Professor," he was onto something. For her part, Misty has said in numerous interviews that she became a bartender after she became disenchanted with the academic world, which is ironic coming from someone who is responsible for educating and training thousands of bartenders around the world. With her cool glasses, half-sleeve tattoo, and authoritative way of speaking, she does have the air of a guest lecturer from the School of Rock.

When I spoke with Misty the first time, she was at home in Boston but about to leave for two weeks in Oaxaca. This is normal—her work for Del Maguey has her visiting *mezcaleros* and taking groups of bartenders around the region for educational tours and training regularly. The Del Maguey model, since Ron Cooper started hauling bottles of hooch in suitcases north to spread the word about this mezcal stuff, has consistently focused on education. Inform the bartenders and the information will trickle down to consumers. For a product like mezcal that truly cannot be sold cheaply *and* ethically, an informed consumer base is essential. For fair trade to be profitable, you need customers to know what "fair" means and why they should pay more for it. Misty seems perfectly suited to this role, for reasons that become more apparent the longer you talk to her.

Misty's hospitality career began as a teenager in her hometown of Green Bay, Wisconsin.

"Actually," she pointed out, "I was born in Mexico, Missouri, so I've kind of come full circle."

Ha!

"When I turned sixteen, my father turned to me and was like, 'Welp! Time to get a job that's not babysitting!' Everybody in my family besides my mother worked in restaurants. We moved to Wisconsin from Missouri when my dad was managing restaurants for Red Lobster. Both my sisters worked in restaurants. So when it was time for me to get a job, I was like, *I guess I'll go to a restaurant!*" She worked in food service until she went to college.

Misty had planned on going to medical school but found she couldn't tolerate the "memorize and regurgitate" curriculum of her biology major. She was making A's in her minor, though, which was religious studies. Misty grew up going to church in Green Bay but said she did not consider herself deeply religious; it was more of an intellectual pursuit. After swapping major and minor, she applied and was accepted to the Harvard Divinity School, which until this interview I did not know was a thing.

The school is part of *that* Harvard, in Boston, and according to its website is "a nonsectarian school of religious and theological studies that educates students both in the pursuit of the academic study of religion and in preparation for leadership in religious, governmental, and a wide range of service organizations." Again, this makes sense. It was training in both critical thinking and community leadership. It was also Misty's entry into the Boston restaurant world.

She started out waitressing; the hours were better than behind the bar. "Then I ended up getting a job in a music club, so that turned into late-night hours no matter what." The next bit sounds like part of a Broadway actor's discovery story: "So one night there a bartender no-showed/no-called during the night of a record release party. They pulled me off the floor and threw me on the bar. I didn't really ever wait tables again after that!" It turned out the bartending schedule, despite the late hours, was even more amenable.

"I didn't have to be in to the music club until 8:00 P.M., and I would be out during the week by 2:00 and on the weekends by 3:00, so it was completely suited to accommodate my class load and actually make some money, because I was poor."

I told her the same thing happened with me, then felt a bit silly, realizing it's the most common story in the business.

The years passed, and Misty found herself increasingly restless in her studies. The academic world lost its appeal. I related to this as well: jumping into what you think is a hallowed intellectual community can end in real disappointment when you discover it is just a workplace, with all the politics and tedium as any other. I can't speak for Misty, but the decision she made upon graduating rang true:

"When I graduated I pretty much knew that I didn't want to be doing what I'd gotten my degree for. I really loved bartending. I loved everything about it. People search their entire lives to find a job that they love, and sometimes they never find it. I felt really fortunate to have it, so it just seemed really stupid to continue on into a PhD program in something that I wasn't really sure that I wanted to do."

After graduating, she was offered a job at the B-Side Lounge, which "was the beginning of the trajectory."

"It was at the B-Side that I met Simon Ford and Bridget Albert, all of these people. Charlotte Voisey. We were one of the few programs in Boston at that point that was using fresh juice and focusing on classic cocktails, and so when national-level ambassadors went to Boston they went to B-Side. It made it possible to meet all of these people and to talk to them about how they got to where they were. That was the key."

Role models. We hear it again and again, and it makes sense; you can't aspire to a position if you don't know it exists or have a clue how to get there. Having people to look up to is everything, so I asked her if she had any particular mentors at the beginning of her career.

"Are you looking specifically for women? Because at that time there weren't a lot of women really doing this." She related the story of how she had at first turned down the job offer at the B-Side Lounge in order to take a summer job in a warmer climate. When she returned, the job was waiting for her, not only because she was good at her job, but because

When I graduated I pretty much knew that I didn't want to be doing what I'd gotten my degree for. I really loved bartending. I loved everything about it. People search their entire lives to find a job that they love, and sometimes they never find it.

"Patrick [Sullivan] couldn't find another woman that was interested in building that style of cocktail." Talk about being your own role model.

Brother Cleve, a musician widely recognized as a kind of John the Baptist of the cocktail scene in Boston, bringing home recipes for strange and delicious cocktails he'd enjoyed on tour, "was the one that taught me about rye whiskey at a time when nobody was talking about rye whiskey. He's obviously a mentor to me. He had to special order a bottle of rye in order to introduce me to it. Patrick Sullivan ended up becoming a business partner of mine. John Gertsen definitely." The infrastructure for the classic cocktail boom was not yet set up in Beantown. Misty and a few friends "put together an organization at the time called the Jack Rose Society. There were four or five of us that would get together and dig into the history of particular classic cocktails, building all the different recipes that we could find to see which ones actually tasted good."

Misty and her cohort of cocktail geeks changed the landscape in Boston. From the B-Side, she went on to bartend at and manage now-famous cocktail dens like Green Street, Drink, and Brick and Mortar, building a reputation for her knowledge of the craft and innovative concoctions.

It was at Green Street that Ron Cooper, founder of Del Maguey Single Village Mezcal, walked in to spy on her. He'd come to town with his bagful of mezcals, looking for allies in his quest to turn the world on to Mexico's original spirit. A friend had told him Misty was the woman to talk to.

Misty told the story of Ron and a friend coming in on a slow night and ordering tequila drinks—whatever she wanted, just make it with tequila. This was 2008, a year before Phil Ward opened Mayahuel in New York to prove that tequila was sophisticated; two years before Las Perlas opened in Los Angeles. Shots of Patron were the fanciest use of agave known to most Americans.

"I'm walking away thinking, *Who the fuck is this guy?* I knew I drank tequila, but *nobody* was drinking tequila at that point in time."

Misty's cocktails were a hit. After his ruse, Cooper introduced himself and brought out some bottles to try. If you remember the mezcal chapter, you can probably predict what happened.

"I was amazed by what I was tasting that night." It was the first time she'd tasted mezcal. They tried a few samples, including a wild *tobalá*. It was the beginning of the next stage in her career, whether she knew it or not.

Misty and Ron became friends, sharing meals and talking about "mezcal and ritual and all these ways that my [divinity] degree was actually tied in to the culture of mezcal. Within a year he invited me to Oaxaca on a trip...

"So I went down with an amazing group of bartenders that was me, Jim Meehan, Phil Ward, Jacques Bezuidenhout, Julio Bermejo...it was a crazy, crazy trip. Then I started helping [Ron] if he needed trainings or anything done in the Boston area. I would go in and do it for him. Just because I believed in what he was doing. I believed in the product, having met the families [that made the mezcal]...I was like, *This is amazing.* So when I got the job with Del Maguey, my friends were like, 'Weren't you already doing that job?' I was like, 'Yeah! They're paying me now, it's so cool!'"

Misty went on the payroll at Del Maguey in 2014 and has since become one of the foremost authorities on mezcal in the United States, particularly the issues surrounding the sustainability of mezcal production. Since the mezcal boom began, over the past seven or eight years the environmental and social impact of its popularity has become a hot issue. Misty is always careful to lay out the environmental, social, economic, and botanical aspects of this somewhat nebulous term, "sustainability."

To this end, she was one of the initial organizers of the Tequila Interchange Project (TIP), a nonprofit advocacy organization made up of "bartenders, consultants, educators, researchers, consumers and tequila enthusiasts" to advocate for "the preservation of sustainable, traditional and quality practices" in the making of agave spirits. The group has been around since 2010, a response to growing concern for how commercial interests might affect the traditional practices of surrounding heritage products. TIP was instrumental in the defeat of one major piece of legislation in Mexico known as NOM 186, the fight against which Sarah Bowen describes beautifully in *Divided Spirits*.

Inspired by her early years tracking down obscure drink recipes with the Jack Rose Society, Misty found another calling.

"LUPEC—Ladies United for the Preservation of Endangered Cocktails—is an organization started in Pittsburgh, Pennsylvania. It is not a bartenders' organization; it is a women's organization. It was started by a group of women . . . who enjoy classic cocktails, who were all interested in women's history. Many had degrees in women's history or had studied women's history...Each month they would get together and they would alternate hosting—twelve women, twelve months. Your job as the host would be to have a cocktail party, and the theme would somehow involve women's history. And throughout, you would pay homage through the cocktails to the women you were highlighting in women's history or the significant time in women's history that you are highlighting. So that's how it started."

A friend from New York, who was not in the industry, tipped Misty off to the group as something she might be into. "And I was like, 'Kitty, let's do this!'" Kitty was Kirsten "Kitty" Amann.

"I reached out to them and asked, 'Would you be interested in having a Boston chapter at all?'" The OG LUPECs assented. "So on the website, there are the articles of incorporation and how to start and all that kind of stuff. I downloaded it and invited a really amazing, diverse group of women. We had a friend of mine who is a water engineer, a friend of mine who was a manager for Zipcar; I had an event planner...obviously some people in the industry as well. So that's how it started. Within the first year, at our first big event we raised over $10,000 for a local women's charity." This was the key component of LUPEC, raising money to "benefit organizations that benefit women in your community or on a larger scale," while bringing attention to delicious libations previously lost to the annals of cocktail history.

The group caught on, and a few different LUPEC chapters sprang up around the country, including New York City, where it became heavily entwined with the Speed Rack crew. The majority of new chapters disappeared as quickly as they arrived, however. When I mentioned this,

Misty clarified: "People don't realize how much work it really is. The events that we would plan, it was like having a second job. All the money goes to charity and that's really amazing, but it's a shit ton of work and it's not just getting together and getting drunk."

After being active with LUPEC for almost a decade, Misty and Kitty have taken their chapter out of the network. They now function as the Toast Club, a name taken from a Boston ladies' organization from the nineteenth century. They wanted to tie the organization to Boston's past in a more meaningful way, preserving its identity as an organization for women inside and outside of the hospitality industry, united in their love of cocktails and desire to give back to their community.

I was introduced to Kirsten "Kitty" Amann by Lynnette Marrero, who was making and serving the drinks at the Dame Hall of Fame ceremony and who was most definitely trying to get rid of me. I do not blame her. In retrospect, sidling up to a busy bartender and announcing you're writing a book on "women in the industry" is completely annoying.

"Have you talked to Kitty about LUPEC?" Lynnette yelled over the excited conversations around us. She indicated a statuesque blond woman in a black sleeveless dress a few yards away. No, I had not. This would soon change. Because once in a room with Kirsten Amann, you can't not talk to Kirsten Amann. She is effervescence embodied.

When I told her what I was up to, bugging all the high-profile women in the room, she said something to the effect of *That's great! We are writing a book about women, too!* Because of my background in literary fiction, her enthusiasm took me aback. When I was in graduate school with a hundred other writers, we all acted friendly and shit-talked relentlessly. But this woman seemed genuinely delighted. I asked her what her book was about.

Kirsten and Misty, in addition to cofounding and running the Toast Club (previously LUPEC Boston), had for years cowritten a weekly column for the Boston publication the *Weekly Dig* (now *DigBoston*), highlighting

Kirsten "Kitty" Amann
Photo Courtesy of Kirsten Amann

unsung women in history with a cocktail recipe. The book based on these columns would be coming out the following spring.

"That's great...," I said, trying to emulate her excitment. Pettiness is a habit that is hard to shake. I asked her what brought her to the event.

"I'm an honoree!" Kirsten replied with genuine glee. My jealousy turned to embarrassment. I'd just asked a guest of honor why she was there. She was unfazed.

If Misty is Boston's rock star professor, Kirsten is the Glinda the Good Witch of New England, but with a glint in her eye. Although Kirsten, like her friend and coauthor Misty, has spent years contributing to the national cocktail community, her beginnings in the industry were ambivalent. After working in restaurants during college at Sarah Lawrence—she planned on being a writer—Kirsten started a promising entry-level job at a publishing house. She could not figure out, however, how all of her colleagues managed to survive in Boston on their salaries.

"Publishing is one of those industries where it just doesn't pay that well, as you probably know. I looked around and was like, *How are people living these lives in this industry?* and then I was like, *Oh, everybody's rich except me. Riiiight.*"

"Rich" as in family money, trust-fund money, spouse-with-a-great-job money.

"I think galleries are the same. You have to hustle if you're not *of means* in that way. So I kind of always did [restaurant work] as a way to make money, and then I got my first publishing job and then I was like, *Oh, I still have to wait tables on the weekend.*"

Being disenchanted with her publishing experience, Kirsten transitioned into a part-time job in public relations when she connected with an "awesome publicist in Boston." She liked the work, but there was little room for growth. "We were doing cookbook PR and it was really fun, and I have a lot of really cool cookbooks from working with all those authors. I learned a lot about marketing, too: the way marketing works in terms of creating someone's brand, and how to do that for other people."

During this time Kirsten was in her later twenties. Her former colleagues were moving up the ladder in their publishing jobs, and she had gone from working full-time and waiting tables on the weekends (sometimes a double on Saturdays...yikes) to working part-time and picking up more bar and restaurant shifts, waiting for her boss's company to grow. She floundered, unsure of which direction to go, feeling entirely dissatisfied.

Redemption came from the unlikeliest source.

"Eventually, what happened was in 2008 the economy died," which shifted her perspective. The situation was dire, and her part-time PR work ended abruptly as clients dropped from her boss's roster.

"It was all so sudden and all so shitty, but my attitude in that moment had just changed dramatically, because everyone I knew was losing their jobs. So these people I had looked around at and been so jealous of, really, who were doing their full-time editorial jobs with higher titles, they all got laid off. Nobody knew what they were going to do, and nobody had side hustle." I should point out that she was not making light of this situation. There was a sense of wonder in her voice at the way things turned out.

"I always would kind of say, offhand, 'Well, if the world all goes to shit I can always bartend!' I said it in this cavalier way...and then it just happened." The source of her prior insecurity—the side hustle that set her apart from her wealthier coworkers—had become her salvation.

Around this same time, she said, she started practicing yoga. "That really helped calm my mind. All the emotional and spiritual benefits of yoga. So I was really having a moment when I was learning about karma and how things happen, whatever, and it helped me reframe everything a little bit." This practice would also come into play later on.

"I had started working in Boston at this place called Toro. It's still to this day one of the best restaurants in the city. And it was just crazy. I went from feeling so frustrated and annoyed to feeling so blessed and just like... holy shit.

"Toro, because of the model, the chef, and the quality of the food... started to get really fantastic. We were making *so* much money. I made more money then in a dead economy than I had before."

I always would kind of say, offhand, 'Well, if the world all goes to shit I can always bartend!' I said it in this cavalier way...and then it just happened.

I understand her fondness. There is something particularly magical about a restaurant that is both lucrative and fun to be in at the same time. It is so rare that we remember these unicorn workplaces forever.

"They were all about education, and I grew so appreciative of that...at night I was getting wine education. We started LUPEC right around then, too, so it felt like I was doing this other meaningful thing."

LUPEC changed Kirsten's perception of the hospitality industry.

"I feel like now it's so different. People who are coming up and getting into the service industry now can have this attitude about it as a career, but back then it wasn't like that. It really wasn't. When I started working in restaurants in 2002, you'd work with these cool, cosmopolitan people, and everybody was an artist or everyone did something else." Before this period, Kirsten had felt less than optimistic about her career choices. She had substantial student loans for Sarah Lawrence and felt dismayed at not following the career she had studied for.

"There was still this air of *Well, what are you doing?* It just didn't feel like restaurants could be a career like they are now." Still, "I was really empowered by both making a lot of money and being in an environment where it was well respected." When she'd meet people from out of town, they would hit her up for unobtainable reservations at her workplace. "It was so weird. I was just this waitress, but everybody cared about that. It was a really fun time in my life."

There are very few things more satisfying than being part of a terrific restaurant team. It is akin to being in a hit play, with people banging down the door to come see you every night, and every night, you prepare to top your previous performances. And if the day was lousy? You have a shift drink, vent, and forget about it. Start over the next night.

Being in a popular, quality establishment helped lift her spirits, and the founding of LUPEC Boston brought Kirsten back to her writing roots. There were a lot of cocktails and women's "forgotten history" that needed to be researched, summed up, and shared. "I had this other twin pursuit, and I did a ton of writing about classic cocktails and cocktail history and I learned so much...so I kind of unwittingly positioned myself as a

I did a ton of writing about classic cocktails and cocktail history and I learned so much... so I kind of unwittingly positioned myself as a knowledgeable person.

knowledgeable person. Not that I wasn't, but you know what I mean. I always held myself in a different esteem because there are so many other people in the city who are great bartenders." Kirsten may not have been a mixology wunderkind, but she created the space for a different type of career for herself.

"Through LUPEC I started networking at different liquor brand events"—these, too, are a much more frequent occurrence these days than when she started. "People are so much more savvy about how to network [now], and they understand what a brand ambassador is. Back then I didn't really know what a brand ambassador was...that I could have that job. I had seen [Hendrick's Gin global ambassador] Charlotte Voisey...I had gone to Tales, so I knew who those really big-name people were, but I didn't realize how many marketing jobs there were in liquor."

While attending events hosted by spirits giant Pernod Ricard, she met the head of marketing in the Boston area, and secured a seasonal position as an ambassador for their English gins, Plymouth and Beefeater.

"[The job] paid well, it was fun...I was basically taking people out for drinks for work and feeling edgy. And doing education, which I loved."

The brand ambassador job is one of the most loved and most reviled among people who have done it. As Kirsten said, the ambassador's job is social, introducing bar staff and consumers to the product, educating them on how it's made and how it can be used. Despite the cultural shift of slow food and small-batch beverages, brand loyalty is still king with liquor brands. While most people are accustomed to asking a waiter for food recommendations, in my bartending experience, getting a patron to try a new spirit requires inordinate trust. Having a charismatic ambassador at the bar buying the rounds might be the quickest way to shift tastes. Imagine: Once this charming individual tells you all about *her* gin and buys you a delicious Eastside cocktail, you begin to wonder what the hell your *old* brand ever did for you.

After the summer stint with Pernod Ricard ended, a friend recommended Kirsten for another brand job with Fernet-Branca. For three and a half years, Kirsten traveled around and preached the word of Branca.

HOPE EWING

This was during a time when the brand's popularity was skyrocketing in the United States, relatively speaking. Fernet-Branca is a traditional Italian *digestivo* in the fernet family of amari, or bitter liqueurs. I highly recommend Brad Thomas Parsons's book *Amaro* if you really want to get down and dirty with what that means. If you've never tried it, Branca is an acquired taste. It is bitter, herbal, sharply minty, and the first time I tasted it I described it as "Satan's mouthwash." The next week, I was drinking it by the shot. That's how it goes with amaro: *This is awful. I'll have another.*

By the early 2010s, Branca became a sort of "bartender's handshake" in most cities in the United States. Ordering a "shot of fernet" at a cocktail bar outed you as a comrade—that is, in my personal experience, someone who had burned their palate out on so much overproof whisky or rum that they needed greater and greater concentrations of flavor in their drinks to stay interested.

But in 2015, she decided to teach yoga full-time. "I'm always kind of vacillating between the liquor business and health and wellness." She still does liquor marketing consulting from time to time, on a freelance basis, and still works with Misty on the Toast Club events and fund-raising.

"It's interesting how these things start out as little baby interests of mine, then they kind of dovetail nicely with how the industry has grown." As the cocktail resurgence approaches its third decade, and bar and liquor jobs become more mainstream and longer lived, attitudes around health and wellness have shifted. For many, it is no longer romantic to overindulge nightly or to revel in how poorly one cares for oneself. Bars have staff wellness trainings. Conferences and festivals offer morning yoga classes and seminars on healthy living and addiction. The previously untouchable subjects of benefits, health care, and the ethics of the tipping system are cropping up as serious discussion points. Kirsten has combined her talents as an expert in liquor, marketing, health, and fitness under one consultancy called "Eat, Drink, Move"—a boozy guru, if you will.

"People's relationship to fitness is very personal. I had people that were like, 'I wanna try yoga but I want to go to *your* class.'" The bar community and the fitness community often have a tense relationship. When your

247

job is, essentially, to provide intoxicants, you can become wary of those whose livelihood is "detoxification." Personally, I live in a town full of therapists and health coaches. Finding one who's not going to tell me to stop drinking and go to bed at the same time every night is a challenge. But the hours, and the liquor tasting, all go with the career. Kirsten was firmly established in both worlds and had special insight into how to use exercise and nutrition to counteract the stress, uneven sleep schedule, and drinking that came with the job.

Kirsten built a private teaching practice aimed at people in hospitality and found clients and support among the Boston restaurant family. Bartenders needed yoga more than most people, she discovered, but they were afraid to get into it for fear they'd be shamed by pristine-livered, well-rested instructors.

Meanwhile, the column for the *Weekly Dig* drew the attention of a literary agent in the late aughts, who thought the pairing of classic cocktail recipes with profiles of famous women would make a "cool book." She and Misty put together a proposal and pitched it but faced rejection after rejection.

"It's funny to look back at it now with all this perspective, because while this was happening, all these other guys who—" She stops to clarify: "Now, Misty is the real deal. She's got a lot of chops in this industry. You know what I mean?" I did. "She came up along so many, so many male bartenders, and she'd come that far by keeping her head down and working twice as hard."

Kirsten continued: "All these—again, not saying anything negative about somebody else—but all these other guys that she came up with were getting book deals. And ours was never sold. So...whatever. It is what it is."

This exasperated phrase always hurts my heart a little bit. "It is what it is." It's the refrain of just about every minority or suppressed population in history: "It is what it is." Until it isn't.

They continued to work on the book in fits and starts until the winter of 2017. In February, another editor reached out to them, having come across the LUPEC Boston blog, which according to Kirsten had not actually been updated in three years.

"He was like, 'I came across your website, I really like it, I think there could be a book there.'...We were like, 'Funny, we have a book proposal!' So we just sent him to our agent."

She didn't want to get her hopes up. It had all happened before, so she remained mellow, did not tell her friends and family that the book was back under review.

"Then, kind of anticlimactically, we got a book deal." *Drinking Like Ladies: 75 Modern Cocktails from the World's Leading Female Bartenders* by Misty Kalkofen and Kirsten Amann would become a reality. Kirsten allowed herself to get a little more excited about the project after presenting to the publishing team. It was a house-wide meeting with the sales force from around the world.

"We just got there, we were like setting up the bar area, and we did a ten-minute presentation, and these people were so awesome and so excited! They came into the room and were like, 'We *love* you guys! We're *so* excited about your book!' After we'd been told so many times that 'we don't get your book, we don't think people will buy it, we don't understand...,' they were like, 'I can't *believe* no one bought this book before.'"

Vindication is best served up with a twist.

10

The Festival Circuit: All Your Faves are Problematic

any of the individuals profiled here were those I met at the 2017 Tales of the Cocktail®, the massive five-day annual cocktail festival held in New Orleans. The first thing you notice about Tales of the Cocktail® is that it is always referred to as Tales of the Cocktail®, so that no one can be in any doubt as to the copyright status of Tales of the Cocktail®. It is the liquor industry equivalent of a music festival mashed up with an international trade summit, with a dash of Burning Man, if all of those things revolved around booze.

The second thing you notice, when you delve into the literature, is that the organization has a hell of a lot of mess to dig itself out of. Even now, as the nonprofit company moves forward with the 2018 festival, the future of the world's biggest booze industry event is uncertain. I had no idea at the time, but when I set off to Tales 2017, I was attending the end of an era.

As the story goes, Tales of the Cocktail began as a walking tour of historic New Orleans cocktail bars in the summer of 2002. The festival grew as the cocktail revival did. By its fifteenth anniversary, its influence was outsize. As Tara Fougner, writing for the publication *Thirsty*, put it: "Much like Fashion Week dictates trends that will eventually hit stores like H&M and TopShop, Tales of the Cocktail highlights the cocktail and beverage trends that will very likely impact what you order the next time that you open up a bar menu." Each year, groups of cocktail enthusiasts swelled the event's ranks until it became what it was in July 2017—the largest bar and liquor industry convention/festival/trade show/rager in the world. Between fifteen and twenty thousand industry folks from around the world descended upon the French Quarter that year, booking in for seminars on history and specialty spirits, countless tastings, partner dinners at NOLA's best restaurants, and oh, those liquor brand parties. Snoop Dogg would be headlining the main Friday night event, and the Spirited Awards—where awards were presented for the world's best bars, bartenders, and brand work—would be hosted by comedian Michael Ian Black. This last bit I thought was an odd choice, since I'd never imagined a connection between Black and the bar world, and his brand of caustic humor seemed out of step with an industry in the middle of a diversity crisis. I suppose it simply meant the Spirited Awards had made it to A-list comedy host territory.

Why this particular festival rose to prominence above all others is up for debate: New Orleans was an ideal setting, with ample local venues for events and plenty of off-season hotel rooms. The efforts of the canny organizers Ann and Paul Tuennerman certainly helped bring in all comers. Tales, as you start calling it once you have to say it more than once, became a rite of passage for "baby bartenders" looking to network or pick up the latest trend of tech to bring back to their home bars. Since 2012, Tales's Dame Hall of Fame has honored influential women in the business each year. It was a great place and time to rub elbows with the new cocktail-era celebrities, as you might find yourself at Arnaud's French 75 one night next to Audrey Saunders or cocktail historian David Wondrich (double swoon!). It was the Comic-Con and the South by Southwest of the cocktail world, as Tara Fougner pointed out, and like both of those festivals, it was already being accused of growing too big for its own good.

My experience at Tales 2017 began in the usual way, from what I have heard. I'd been warned about "blowing my load" on the first day and nursing a hangover for the rest of the festival. This I was determined to ward off. I was already north of thirty and well acquainted with the three-day hangover. Before taking off for New Orleans, I went shopping and made a plan. I packed a mobile pharmacy of plant extracts and electrolyte supplements, an extra-large water bottle, and healthy snacks and pinkie-swore with my photographer/boyfriend, Tuan Lee, that we would control ourselves.

Of course, we know what both the Yiddish proverb and Scots poet Robert Burns had to say about plans. Both were all too true.

Tuan and I took off on Wednesday morning—the second day of the festival. I was already running on financial fumes, even with my media passes, and was hoping that saving one night's hotel fees would help. I regretted the late arrival as soon as we walked in the Hotel Monteleone looking for the media registration room. The lobby was swarming with people of all ages and levels of dress formality, of varying levels of drunkenness and volume of voice. We had walked into the party two drinks behind everyone else.

We located the registration desk and grabbed our badges. Our tempers were short from early rising and air travel. The afternoon's events were wrapping up, and women in traditional Peruvian dress exited a nearby conference room, followed by more tottering attendees. I panicked slightly, wondering if we had missed everything important. I was armed with a list of events to attend and people to interview, as well as restaurants to hit up, and had no idea how we were going to accomplish it all.

"Sustainability" was a buzzword at the 2017 festival, and although we were not in a full-blown nationwide sexual assault awareness campaign yet, the cocktail community had at least begun to wake up about this topic. Paper straws had replaced plastic, and several seminars attempted to tackle issues of bar waste and sexual assault. This was progress, I thought, dubiously swigging from my second of infinite complimentary plastic bottles of spring water stockpiled in bins all around the Monteleone's lobby, washing down an amaro sample from one of the hundreds of little plastic cups I'd toss away through the course of the week.

We swung over to a nearby restaurant to catch the end of the Girls with Bols annual reunion, hosted by the beverage company Lucas Bols and featuring bartender Kate Gerwin, whom I wanted to stalk. Bols is the producer of, among other things, Bols Genever, a Dutch spirit considered the predecessor of English gin. It's light and juniper-y, but often has a maltier quality—a hint of toasted Cheerios, if you will. Kate was the first woman and first American to win the Bols Around the World bartending competition in 2014. She then founded Girls with Bols (get it?) as a mentorship program, pairing women industry vets with the next generation of women bartenders. We arrived toward the end of the event, having dashed off to our hotel to offload luggage and grab some much-needed food. Kate was behind the bar, supervising and serving up the menu of genever-based delights.

She is imposing—tall, tattooed, and fuchsia-haired, looking very much like a cool rocker girl I would have had a secret friend crush on in high school but never would have spoken to. Born in Northern California, she grew up all over the United States, returning to Napa Valley at age twenty-one to learn winemaking. She'd been working in restaurants since she was a teenager and had developed a passion for wine. After living and working in Napa for a few years, she went to New Mexico to open a restaurant, and in doing so she taught herself cocktail craft. Kate describes herself as a self-taught bartender, having worked in restaurants around the country her entire adult life, but rarely in major cities like San Francisco or New York where she would have the advantage of mentorship from the established cocktail programs there.

When she won the Bols competition, she was running a multivenue bar, restaurant, and retail concept in Bismarck, North Dakota. She's consulted in Las Vegas, teaches at culinary schools, and recently opened a new bar in Santa Cruz, California. Kate Gerwin is a boss, and she brings her own star power.

She was busy when I finally got her attention. I asked if I could chat with her later in the week about her career, creating cocktail scenes outside of the usual markets. We exchanged information and made tentative plans to connect the following day. Had I ever been to Tales before, I would not have been so easygoing about this. By the time I had poked my head up from my three-day dust devil of interviews and events, she had left town.

The festival, honestly, blurs together, and not just from the alcohol. After immediately losing my resolve to stay sober during the first evening's brand parties, on the second day I met with gin producers from London and did my best to enjoy their signature martini while my body was screaming out for Gatorade. After that, a New York City rye producer. More walking, more tasting. More water. I gobbled down finger foods at a mingling event thrown by spirits distributor Southern Glazer's and dreamed about naps I would never take. I attended the "Toast to Herstory" cocktail competition, sponsored by the Marie Brizard liqueur company. Bartenders from all over the country had submitted cocktail recipes inspired by famous women, and five had been selected to receive a free trip to Tales to showcase their drinks for festival attendees to vote on. There were cocktails honoring urban planning activist Jane Jacobs, actress Rita Moreno, and Lisa Simpson, among others.

I met with producers of bourbon and mezcal, admired the fabulousness of the restaurants taken over and lavishly redecorated by Absolut and Campari. There was a theme park quality to the brands' efforts. The current running through it all was cash money, and it ran hot. As a bartender I was thrilled that companies would spend so much to impress us. As a human being, it put me in a bit of a funk.

I could not have told you at the time what specifically was bugging me, but in retrospect I see. Everything involving the city of New Orleans was a delight. Almost everything involving the actual festival fell somewhere between taxing and terrifying. There were just too many people, too many events, too much hustle in one space. I've never been a great hustler, preferring to nerd out in depth with a few similarly interested folks rather than litter the room with business cards (note: I neglected to make business cards; I'm not a real person yet). Over the following two days I attended two meet-the-distillers-type events and collected dozens of cards and a backpack full of branded key rings, tote bags, lip balm tubes, buttons, you name it. Gin was big in the tasting rooms, and grappa was being marketed as the next big new cocktail ingredient. I talked to women founders, brand owners, and ambassadors who held forth tirelessly, valiantly. I realized this was a great place to see the bartenders you admired but the worst place to actually talk to them. Everyone was just so busy. There was excitement but also desperation. We all so poignantly wanted this to be worth it.

The highlights of the festival were, for me, Gin World (where I met Melissa Katrincic and saw Natasha Bahrami in action) and the Dame Hall of Fame induction ceremony, which I have already spoken of at length. I was in a state of awe at seeing all the women I'd read so much about. In addition to Kirsten Amann, ms. franky marshall, and Joy Spence, the women honored that night were Sharon Bronstein, vice president of marketing for the 86 Company; Detroit bartender Dorothy Elizabeth, another chemist turned mixologist; and Katy Casbarian of New Orleans's storied Arnaud's French 75 restaurant. I became their immediate fan, seeing how this group seemed to have each other's backs. Even so, there was an indefinable sense of unease among the attendees. It would be a few months before I could make a guess as to why.

In the spring of 2017, months before I was schmoozing it up with the exhausted gentry of the cocktail world, the controversy had already begun. That year at Mardi Gras, Tales founder Ann Tuennerman and her husband, Paul, rode in the parade of the Zulu Krewe, a historic New Orleans social and philanthropic club. The Tuennermans had been invited by the Zulu organization and, following the group's tradition, donned blackface makeup and wigs for the event. This would have been a PR headache to begin with, but one easily explained away (to many people) by the fact that everyone, black and white, was wearing blackface on that float, and it was one of those local idiosyncrasies people from NOLA know as a part of their traditions. What truly ignited a storm of bad press was the video Ann posted on social media, quoting her husband, stating, "Throw on a little blackface, lose all your Media Skills." What exactly did Paul intend by this? Was he poking fun at his wife's awkwardness or insulting African Americans' media skills? People—industry folks, the beverage press, and the friends and community of the Tuennermans—were dumbstruck. Then the couple's response made things worse—a series of non-apology apologies.

As the community's anger grew, Ann announced Paul would be leaving the organization, and Tales of the Cocktail would form a "diversity council" comprising high-profile industry people of color, to better address issues of discrimination, representation, and opportunities for people of color in the industry. For a few months, it seemed like some actual progress could come from the whole ugly ordeal. Tales had been criticized in the past for its relative quiet on these topics; perhaps this would be looked back at as a teachable moment.

But shortly after Tales 2017, Ann announced that Paul was back in. Not only was she bringing him back to his leadership role within the Tales organization, but she also revealed in an email that he had remained 50 percent owner of MOJO 911, the production company that ran and profited from the whole affair. Additionally, word came out that the diversity council had met only once in seven months and hadn't been given any clear statement of purpose. This was the final nail in the Tuennermans' Tales coffin.

Even before the controversial video, there had been grumblings about Tales's worth to brands, bartenders, and the rest. Amanda Schuster, writing for the *Alcohol Professor* in 2017, expressed her ambivalence at the decline of a festival that had helped her build her career as a writer, since she had met the publication's editor there years earlier. Tales remained the biggest liquor industry event of the year, the best place for making connections. Even writing this now feels a bit like biting the hand that fed me, as I myself have written for the Tales publication. The festival has always been touted as a huge boon for the summertime tourism economy of New Orleans, a city everyone agrees not only has a fantastic drinking history and culture, but has had enough hard knocks in recent decades. But increasingly, as Camper English pointed out in a piece for *SevenFifty Daily* published one month after the 2017 conference, brands and individuals were questioning the return on investment of the event.

Individual attendance, with tickets, lodging, and flights, could run well over $1,000. Branded events such as the sponsored "Spirited Dinner" series could run in the tens of thousands. The payoffs—exposure, greater national recognition—could be hard to quantify. Many industry vets were concluding that the festival held little benefit left for them, saying that spaces were typically reserved for younger colleagues. These young ones would often return from New Orleans talking about the spectacle of the event rather than new knowledge or techniques.

As this came out, the beverage media continued to uncover unsavory details from the Tuennermans' reign. Tara Fougner published in *Thirsty* part of a tax document that showed that the director and executive director of the company had received over $840,000 each in "professional fees" the previous year through MOJO 911. Tales of the Cocktail had long been touted as an organization dedicated to supporting the people of New Orleans, but clearly much of that support was directed at two people in particular.

I will add that I dropped $180 for two tickets to the Dame Hall of Fame two-hour passed hors d'oeuvres event, and though I don't regret it (the cocktails were fantastic), it irks me a bit now to think about the Tuennermans' yacht and how many festival presenters reported being pressured to "donate" their speaking fees. In fact, after the 2017 event, four of the Dame Hall of Fame founding members—Misty Kalkofen, Kirsten Amann, Lynnette Marrero, and Meaghan Dorman—resigned from the group. Speed Rack, the all-women bartending competition, severed official ties with Tales of the Cocktail, aligning closely in 2018 with a new cocktail festival premiering that May in Chicago called Chicago Style. Chicago Style was organized by prominent industry women: Caitlin Laman of the Ace Hotel in Chicago, Shelby Allison of Chicago's Lost Lake bar, and 2017 Dame inductee Sharon Bronstein of the 86 Company. Dissent had been building quietly for a while.

Shortly after the news came out, the following September, that Ann Tuennerman had rehired her husband without consulting the very council that was formed to advise her, diversity council cochair Colin Asare-

Appiah walked away, issuing a statement that he would be supporting the mission of diversity from "outside of the Tales of the Cocktail organization."

Days later, both Ann and Paul resigned and relinquished control of the festival and the production company they'd held for fifteen years. Tales of the Cocktail was sold to the Solomon family, New Orleans philanthropists with ties to the hospitality community. As of this writing, the organization has sent out a call for proposals as a grant-making body and is publicly reframing itself as a nonprofit organization. The festival is set to go on as planned in July 2018.

I echo the ambivalence of my fellow drinks writers. For as painful as I found the entire affair at times, between the crowds, the packed scheduling, the expense, and the FOMO, many of the women I've included in this volume are those I met there, and several count the Tales of the Cocktail Apprentice Program as an important part of their training. It feels a shame to lose the positive aspects because of some shady behavior by those in charge. Perhaps the cocktail world has grown too large for one mega-event to suffice. Personally, I think we can spread the cocktail love between a few festivals. I join my hopeful comrades in wishing the new Tales of the Cocktail administration the best of luck.

I arrived at Chicago Style at the end of its first day, because it was a last-minute decision, and I'm me. Truth be told, I was risking the wrath of my editorial team by stretching my final draft submission precious days past deadline. This seemed important enough to risk it, though. From the press that heralded the festival as a hard look at the industry's social problems—sexual assault, racism, sexism, and environmental impact—to the caliber of the presenters and sponsors, this first-time conference felt like exactly the right place to be if I wanted to get a glimpse into the future. Also, the national finals of Speed Rack were there, and I really wanted to see who won. I hit the ground at O'Hare with enough time to drop my bags off at my cousin's house in Edgewater and hop on the L down to the

Speed Rack finals in the West Loop. It was my first time in Chicago, but my New Yorker's superpower of public transit navigation got me there right on time.

Much like the regional finals I'd attended in San Francisco the previous November, this year's national competition was held in a cavernous event space, with sponsor booths flanking all sides of the room slinging punch and branded schwag and a stage front and center for the contestants and judges. The judges this year were Julie Reiner, David Wondrich, London bar innovator Ryan Chetiyawardana, and festival organizer (and Ms. Speed Rack 2014) Caitlin Laman. In a bracket-style throwdown, two competitors went head-to-head, making four drinks simultaneously. Each judge requested a cocktail, which included everything from a Remember the *Maine* to an espresso martini to David Wondrich's request for a *batanga* (tequila and Coke, mixed with a knife, preferably one that has been used to make guacamole, as invented by Don Javier Delgado Corona of the La Capilla bar in the town of Tequila), and the eager competitors hustled to make the four drinks as quickly and accurately as possible. They would be judged on their speed, but also their technique and, above all, the balance and tastiness of their drinks.

One way in which Speed Rack differs from other cocktail competitions is that the judges give their feedback directly to the contestants, who stand together on the stage to receive the news. Scores start off as the time it takes to complete the multistep cocktails from pour to garnish, and they receive additions of between five and thirty seconds for flaws such as under- and overshaking, wrong proportion of ingredients, and improper garnishing. The other key thing that sets this contest apart is that all the competitors are women.

Founded in 2011 by New York bartenders Ivy Mix and Lynnette Marrero, Speed Rack was created as an answer to what they saw as chronic underrepresentation of female talent in similar competitions and in the leadership of the bar world at large. It was a daring move to create what could be seen as a segregated space, considering how hard many women fight for recognition as equals and disdain being considered what

Mary Bartlett called "the girl version of [their] job." But Mix and Marrero wanted to bring together large numbers of women at the top of their field, creating a career-fostering environment. With their steadfast management of the process, which this year included a bonding trip to Jalisco for all the regional finalists, it has turned into what seems like the most supportive love-fest competition in history. If I had any trepidations about making women compete against one another, this thought had well been accounted for and dismissed. Paired up onstage, after all the mixing and shaking are done, contestants are often seen holding hands as they wait for the judges' feedback, and the disqualified reappear to cheer on their defeaters in subsequent rounds. Pre- and post-competition interviews show bartenders who want to win but who also seemed pumped just to be there. It seems, too, that the organizers' goal of promoting female talent has succeeded; past participants Lacy Hawkins (who made it to the final round an incredible five times before winning the title in 2016), LA's Yael Vengroff, Houston's Alba Huerta, Caitlin Laman, and Chicago's Mony Bunni have gone on to prominent careers all over the world. It appears that despite being ladies only, being a Speed Rack winner connotes serious chops in multigender arenas.

Over the past seven years, the competition has reportedly raised around $800,000 for breast cancer charities. There are times when this mission hits close to home, as during the California regionals for season seven, when all the Los Angeles-based spectators showed up in T-shirts with TEAM BROOKE stenciled on them. Brooke Arthur, a bar star who has made a name for herself all over the West Coast, was at the time fighting her own cancer battle. For an industry that rarely touts health insurance as one of its perks, the charitable aspect was far from abstract.

Tears are a common sight on the Speed Rack stage, as the "no crying in baseball" mentality of so many bars and boardrooms very firmly does not apply. In this woman-centric space, it seems, expressions of emotion are normalized. Season seven came to a particularly tearful conclusion. After New York's Haley Traub beat out local Chicago favorite Katie Renshaw for the Ms. Speed Rack 2018 title, participants Mary Palac, Natalie Ledesma,

Madelyn Kay, and Araya Anderson took the stage to cut off their hair as an extra fund-raising push. They'd raised an additional $4,000 already and were collecting donations and bids on who would wield the scissors. Palac, Ledesma, and Kay lost upward of seven inches each of waist-length hair to donate for wigs for chemotherapy patients, while Anderson had her San Francisco mentor Brooke Arthur take the stage to shave her head to a quarter of an inch in solidarity. Everyone was crying, male, female, and nonconforming, partly because haircuts are always a bit traumatic, but mostly due to the overwhelming beauty of women supporting one another. I threw a few bills into the basket as it passed and sipped on my *copita* of Del Maguey mezcal that Misty Kalkofen had poured from her sponsor table. I was struck with pride at how California and Texas had represented the states' strong Pacific Islander and Latina heritage, and how all the finalists seemed laser focused on the fund-raising aspect of the event. From this vantage point, the future was female, and it was fantastic.

The next day, I sipped the conference's signature mocktail (possibly my favorite innovation) when Ashtin Berry took the floor to present "Community Accountability: All Your Faves Are Problematic." Berry's seminar was the second of day two of Chicago Style's official programing, held at the Ace Hotel in the West Loop. Other seminars focused on topics such as bar waste management, sexual assault and harassment prevention, and, above all, bringing the cocktail community together to hear from those who don't typically get a platform.

Earlier, Colin Asare-Appiah (of Bacardi USA, formerly of the Tales of the Cocktail Diversity Council) led a presentation with the leaders of the Chicago-based nonprofit Causing a Stir, Alexis Brown and Ariel E. Neal. The three explored the organization's efforts to support underrepresented communities within the bar industry, particularly in Chicago's historically African American South Side. From there, presenters spoke on the industry's responsibility to its respective communities and on the history of black bartenders. By the time I joined the party, we were on to environmental impact with the Trash Collective—a Toronto-based consultancy that helps create low-waste bars—and leaders of prominent programs around the country who have taken steps to eliminate common sources of pointless bar waste. The vibes were good. Then Ashtin Berry came on the scene and took us to school.

Sadly, words like "feminism" and "intersectionality" can still tune a lot of folks out. It's a mean irony that bringing up "inclusivity" can make something feel limited to the ranks of academics and activists. When Ashtin took the floor at the Ace's events room, she made sure all eighty or so participants were engaged, requiring audible confirmation of her questions, right down to "How are you doing?" She told us she incorporates a lot of call-and-response in her speaking work. Ashtin is the beverage curator at Tokyo Record Bar in New York City, and though her roots are in Philadelphia, she worked in the bar industry in Chicago and New Orleans before winding up in NYC. Slight and striking, Berry projected an edgy, academic vibe, dressed in a hip T-shirt and slacks ensemble with a mass of braids pulled up on top of her head and trailing down her back. Her posture betrayed a dance background, which the internet confirmed. All these things helped her achieve perfect command of the room as she guided us through some complex ideas and a whole lot of real talk.

The presentation was eye-opening, not because I was unfamiliar with the concepts she presented like tokenism, stereotyping, and implicit bias—I live in Los Angeles and hang out almost exclusively with psychology and sociology grads—but because she had such detailed instructions for how workplace communities can get better at supporting their most vulnerable members. She split the room into four groups, and we each worked through a different scenario where someone in the hospitality business was put in an uncomfortable or dangerous position because of their race, gender, or sexuality. For instance, my group, comprising cis men and women from different parts of the country and different ethnic backgrounds, discussed how a gender-nonconforming person of color could navigate the very white, very gendered dress code requirements of a potential job offer. The kicker was, of course, that every sample scenario was taken from real life. Our troubling hypotheticals were someone else's realities. We additionally were instructed to variously "hang back/step up"—that is, go against our usual tendency to either bow out of or dominate the discussion, so that those who usually stay silent were made to lead.

I left the seminar charged up. Here were some real tools I could use in my own workplaces to better communicate with people with different backgrounds from mine, here were realistic tools to make change. It also left me with a sinking sensation regarding my almost, almost, *almost* done manuscript for this book. Had I really done enough to be inclusive? Probably not.

My biggest regret in this volume is the omission of many incredible women and gender-nonconforming folks due to space, time, snowstorms, and missed opportunities. Most poignantly I want to acknowledge the relative dearth of women of color. I set out to boost the visibility of "women making waves" because I believe seeing someone who looks like or has a similar background as yourself excelling in your field can act as a lodestar. *If they can do it, so can I.* I fear, nearing the end, that I've failed to include enough of those whom L. A. McCrae called the "us-es" of this world. This reflects partly the imbalanced state of the industries themselves and partly authorial shortcomings. I am keenly aware of the specter of tokenism, the inclusion of a bare minimum of underrepresented people, and stopping there, well short of real change.

People more marginalized than I am are courageously storming the gates in the booze industry. I am grateful that Chicago Style came into being to introduce a wider audience to organizations like Causing a Stir, which had not appeared on any deep research dive I'd attempted. It is a conscientious consumer's responsibility to support them with our social media attention and purchase dollars, and I've made an effort to include more than a token's worth in the recommended drinking and reading sections. It is our responsibility to keep trying to be better.

11

Our #MeToo Moment

I t barely registered in the national press, but the bartending community had its own "Weinstein moment" in October 2016. It happened over a year before women in entertainment, public service, media, and tech came forward to call out powerful men who had used their positions to manipulate and abuse, and the world finally, finally saw fit to believe them.

The year before the Revolution of 2017, as I've come to think of it, a prominent West Coast bartender who cofounded one of the country's most sought-after consultancies posted a fare-thee-well missive on his Facebook page. This individual had a dream job, from all appearances, hopping from city to city setting up hot new bar programs, training staff, and spreading the gospel of the craft cocktail renaissance while repping cool liquor brands. Like Harvey Weinstein, this man was physically daunting. Tall and broad with a booming voice and the energy of a true bon vivant, he was at once magnetic and somewhat terrifying. He had a huge network and was spoken of as someone to know if one wanted to join the ranks of cocktailers on the rise.

His good-bye-to-all-this post was not altogether unexpected; after being at the top of the game for a while, it's a common trajectory to sober up or burn out. All the partying had run him down, he wrote; he'd behaved poorly and he was leaving town to start over with his wife and children. He apologized vaguely to anyone he might have hurt during his darker days.

The comments poured in: well wishes, declarations of support, solidarity, and love. For a number of industry women, however, his sweeping admission was a fresh insult. Within days, a Wordpress site appeared called the Reality of Sexual Assault in the Cocktail Community, expressing this frustration:

> It's hard to explain the emotions that we felt when our assailant posted a public apology to the cocktail community for "effecting/hurting/insulting" anyone due to their actions under the influence of drugs and alcohol. We were (again) hurt and discounted from a sincere apology that should conceivably be face to face.

The fifteen women who came forward had been repeatedly assaulted and harassed by this man, and any relief at his leaving the industry for good was offset by the "800 likes and 200 comments that read 'I love you,' and 'You are so strong'" that followed his "apology." Some signed their accounts with initials, others posted anonymously, but a good number posted their names. Most were prominent bartenders and directors in Los Angeles, Portland, and San Francisco. They cataloged stories of abuse and assault spanning years. Of being choked in their own bars after hours. Of being restrained and pawed at while they fought to free themselves. Of feeling unable to tell anyone without risking their careers. The craft cocktail world, for all its flamboyant press, is a small one. This person mentored hundreds of young bartenders. He was not, as he characterized himself, a victim of the drug and alcohol abuse. He was a serial predator, drunk or sober.

This man was not charged with anything, and because of libel laws, his name was not published in any of the accounts. But again, this isn't a huge community. Word quietly got around, heads shook, and commiserations and near misses were recounted. Those who gave their names were known as straight-talking, jocular bosses. Those outside of his inner circle just could not believe it. Then, a little too quickly, we stopped talking about it.

I've often wondered why that moment passed relatively unnoticed, while other industries' stories blew a hole in the status quo. There is the question of reach, sure—this was a big regional man, not an international celebrity. But there is no doubt in my mind that the stigma of the "drinking woman" played a huge role in these stories being suppressed or written off. As Fred Minnick notes in *Whiskey Women*, the intractable business partners of whiskey and prostitution in the brothels of the nineteenth century influenced American ideas about women who drink long past when Prohibition ran the industry underground. Even now, in the catalog of victim-blaming inquiries, "How much did you have to drink?" pops up like a boil when women call out their abusers. An interesting factoid from a National Institute on Alcohol Abuse and Alcoholism publication cites "stereotypes about drinking women being sexually available and appropriate targets" as a factor exploited by would-be rapists. Despite our desire to appear impervious, we may need to recognize that predators seek out alcohol professionals as well as "drunk girls" because they—and many times, we—think *no one will believe us*.

Just over a year later, after the world woke to the reality and ubiquity of this kind of harassment, another prominent barman was accused of assaulting female colleagues. This time, a police report was filed, and celebrity bartender Marcos Tello was accused of multiple instances of rape, assault, and misconduct. The alleged victims' accounts were reported in visceral detail by the online publication *Neat Pour*, an indication to me that the industry was finally gunning for those who had been the subject of "whisper networks" for years. The bar community could be ready to face its own demons.

On one level, we are adamant about protecting customers from compromising situations. Training on assault prevention and how to run interference for a guest suffering unwanted attention from another guest is easily accessible online and discussed at industry events. We have long been done with the idea that drinking in public marks a woman. Except, it seems, with our own. Admitting that the general public is full of creeps who use alcohol as a date rape drug is one thing; recognizing the capacity for this among our peers and mentors is quite another. We can only hope that in this new "woke" climate, women will no longer fear not being believed and that reporting abuse will not jeopardize their own career.

The fact that bar/restaurant workers are mostly part-time, with no job security, and are generally seen as both itinerant and replaceable only complicates things further. A study by the Restaurant Opportunities Centers United reported in 2016 that 78 percent of servers and bartenders surveyed reported being harassed by customers. As long as the income is tip based, service pros will feel the pressure to grin and bear it as long as they can. With all the possible threats coming in from outside, a little semi-joking harassment from a coworker can feel like the least of one's worries. It's a hard case to make that we have to desexualize the workplace, but a necessary one.

Within the last couple of years, calls have become increasingly audible for change and accountability, especially as work in booze-related professions gains legitimacy as lifelong career material. Since the public outing of celebrity chefs like John Besh and Mario Batali and, of course, bartender/accused rapist Marcos Tello as predators in the workplace, the tight-knit hospitality world faces a reckoning. Catch up and take a real look at sexual harassment and assault. Stop using alcohol as an excuse.

Prominent liquor community figure Brooke Arthur, writing on the Reality of Sexual Assault in the Cocktail Community, summed it up: "The abuse of alcohol and drugs creates a petri dish of shame," wherein feelings about "overindulgence, confusion, promiscuity, and fear...keep us from protecting each other from these inexcusable offenses. AND I'M OVER IT."

We are so over it.

Garnish

Reflections on Moving and Shaking

To paraphrase Dickens: the booze world is hella ambivalent right now. It is heartening to see the impressive progress brought about by women like Teri Fahrendorf, Deborah Brenner, Ivy Mix, and Lynnette Marrero. It's tempting to start feeling pretty proud, until another story of harassment and discrimination reminds us of how very far there is left to go. Having spent so much time thinking about the idea of progress in these industries, I can't say I have come away with any clear concept of what lies ahead. I do feel like the culture is more aware of bias and less tolerant of gross behavior, and that the hypermasculine ethos that bullied too many promising female talents out of many high-profile bars is becoming less and less common. I delight each week in finding a new woman-made booze to enjoy, and as many have said in the preceding pages, things are looking up.

One question kept nagging me, though, and as a side note, I needed to settle this. The more people I spoke to, the more the year 2008 seemed to come up. The formation of the Pink Boots Society. Alice Feiring's whistle-blowing on wine cellar doctoring. The year craft cocktail culture finally seemed to break nationwide. It was almost uncanny. I wanted so badly to tie these boozy revolutions to the inspiration of the Obama years. The reality is less happy. When I asked people why 2007–2009 seemed to be such a red-letter couple of years, they were more likely to cite the onset of recession than any burgeoning sense of hope and change. It's been ten years now since the economy tanked so majestically, sending countless laid-off professionals to follow their passions for beer/wine/whisky/ etc. Ten years since a generation discovered, as Kirsten Amann did, that the white-collar path doesn't necessarily pay the bills any better than our service industry roots. Bartending became a career, not just a gig. The economy recovered, mostly, and interest in things that are high quality, locally produced, and made with care spread even wider. And finally, ten years in, it feels as if women are beginning to be taken seriously as players in this world.

The connection between natural wine, craft booze, and cocktails and social awareness is obvious: much of the philosophy is actually about simplification. You use plant- or animal-made fertilizers for grape vines rather than lab-concocted petroleum-based ones. You brew beer you and your friends want to drink and serve it in a welcoming community space, or you squeeze a lemon into a cocktail instead of spraying a mixture of citric acid and corn syrup. These are all innovations and simplifications. What I would like to propose is that removing bias against women is as clear and obvious a choice as removing pesticides and artificial coloring. We don't need it, and our products and lives would all benefit from its banishment.

The industry changes helped along by the women in this book all involved a philosophy of care, of paying attention. The booze industries vary hugely, but giving a damn about what does and doesn't go into one's product is the clear common denominator among all those profiled here. The next logical step on this path is paying attention to whom these industries benefit and whom they leave out. Terroir is about the soil, climate, and microbes, but it's also about the "hand of the maker." *Who* makes the wine, beer, or spirit is as important as *what* makes it.

So to answer the question once and for all, so that it need never be asked again: What *is* it like to be a woman in the alcohol business?

I lost track of it myself for a bit. I quit bartending to write this. I had decided it was time to move on—enough with the erratic hours, the unpredictable pay, the drunk-kid coworkers. When I was about ten pages from the end, I started up again. I missed it so much: the camaraderie, the adrenaline, and most of all that feeling you get when you serve someone something they absolutely love. Late bloomer as always, I became the junior bartender at a chef-driven (read: nerdy) joint at the age of thirty-seven. Up until now I could pass for younger. This was the year that stopped happening, and my coworkers look at me quizzically as the weird older broad who's hanging around in their world. This does not faze me as I thought it would, mostly because having spoken to all the women profiled here, I feel a renewed sense that I can do whatever the hell I want and be great at it. I now have plenty of role models to choose from.

More generally, though, we've learned what it is like for thirty of us, so here goes. It is keeping your head down, working hard, and having a thick skin. It's organizing, believing each other, and giving back to your community. It's about doing flawless work that can't be ignored and finding the support of like-minded friends. One thing to note from this collection of experiences is that even women who've faced no outright abuse or discrimination have stories of having to fight harder to be heard, respected, or given their due. We take this for granted, just as we accept that we must be exponentially more talented and capable than cis male counterparts to achieve the same levels of success. But now "It is what it is" isn't enough anymore.

Being a woman in the industry is a raucous competition to see who can make the best, fastest daiquiri. It's mentorship and standing up for one another and setting up systems to enable education for those who crave it. It's calling out predators and learning how to protect our guests from them; it's making safe community spaces for the "us-es." It's facing horrifying levels of institutional abuse and keeping going. It is fun, fascinating, infuriating, delicious, back-breaking, exhausting, friend-for-life-making, scary, awe-inspiring, tedious, and, above all, intoxicating work. For the women who make and serve our social lubricants, it's been a long time coming, but in many ways, we're just getting started.

Recommended Reading

Baiocchi, Talia. *Sherry: A Modern Guide to the Wine World's Best-Kept Secret, with Cocktails and Recipes*. Berkeley, CA: Ten Speed Press, 2014.

In her first book, Baiocchi undertakes her own journey of discovery to Jerez, Spain, delving into the production of this erstwhile misunderstood fortified wine.

————, and Leslie Pariseau. *Spritz: Italy's Most Iconic Aperitivo Cocktail, with Recipes*. Berkeley, CA: Ten Speed Press, 2016.

The *Punch* editors explore the history and modern applications of these low-abv, bittersweet fizzy cocktails.

Bowen, Sarah. *Divided Spirits: Tequila, Mezcal, and the Politics of Production*. Oakland: University of California Press, 2015.

Written from her time as a graduate student in Jalisco and Oaxaca, Bowen's definitive work on the subject of agave spirits is at once rigorously academic and captivating to read.

Burian, Natalka, and Scott Schneider. *A Woman's Drink: Bold Recipes for Bold Women*. New York: Chronicle Books, 2018.

A cocktail book for the contemporary woman, featuring recipes inspired by Burian's bars Elsa and Ramona, and including favorite drinks from notable women.

Cheever, Susan. *Drinking in America: Our Secret History.* New York: Twelve, 2016.

A literary scholar of addiction and recovery, Cheever takes us through the United States' fraught history with intoxicating beverages with thoroughness and wit.

Feiring, Alice. *The Battle for Wine and Love: Or, How I Saved the World from Parkerization.* Boston, MA: Mariner Books, 2008.

———. *For the Love of Wine: My Odyssey through the World's Most Ancient Wine Culture.* Lincoln, NE: Potomac Books, 2016.

———. *Naked Wine: Letting Grapes Do What Comes Naturally.* Cambridge, MA: Da Capo Press, 2011.

———, and Pascaline Lepeltier. *The Dirty Guide to Wine: Following Flavor from Ground to Glass.* New York: Countryman Press, 2017.

She claimed she will never write another wine book, so in the meantime enjoy Feiring's deeply personal stories of searching out "untampered-with" vino from France to Spain to the Republic of Georgia, even stopping to make her own vintage in the middle of "Parker country," California. She collaborated for the final text with superstar sommelier Lepeltier for a deep dive into the dirt-and-stones aspect of terroir.

Gaytán, Marie Sarita. *¡Tequila! Distilling the Spirit of Mexico.* Stanford, CA: Stanford University Press, 2014.

Sociology professor Gaytán takes us through the history of tequila in Mexico, what it means to the nation's identity, and how it is changed by and affects contemporary culture.

Greene, Heather. *Whisk(e)y Distilled: A Populist Guide to the Water of Life.* New York: Avery, 2015.

Spirits somm and whiskey educator Greene was the first American woman to serve in the Scotch Malt Whisky Society in Edinburgh. Her plainspoken dissection of whisk(e)y lore and tasting methods are beginner-friendly, but even an expert should appreciate her breadth of knowledge and fascinating stories.

Hoffman, Maggie. *The One-Bottle Cocktail: More Than 80 Recipes with Fresh Ingredients and a Single Spirit*. California: Ten Speed Press, 2018.
Former *Serious Eats* editor Hoffman brings together eighty recipes from bartenders all over the country that incorporate easily accessible ingredients for the home bartender and only one spirit. An absolute staple at any vacation house or home bar.

Huerta, Alba, and Marah Stets. *Julep: Southern Cocktails Refashioned*. California: Lorena Jones Books, 2018.
Houston bartender and Speed Rack alumna Huerta brings recipes and stories together to tell an affectionate history of drinking in the American South.

Janzen, Emma. *Mezcal: The History, Craft & Cocktails of the World's Ultimate Artisanal Spirit*. Minneapolis, MN: Voyageur Press, 2017.
Imbibe magazine writer Janzen takes a cocktail-centric look at Mexico's ancestral spirit in this volume, with novice-friendly accounts of the spirit's history and production.

Kalkofen, Misty, and Kirsten Amann. *Drinking Like Ladies: 75 Modern Cocktails from the World's Leading Female Bartendersy*. Beverly, MA: Quarry Books, 2018.
Kalkofen and Amann, founders of the Boston chapter of Ladies United in the Preservation of Endangered Cocktails (LUPEC) and the Toast Club, collect stories of underappreciated women in history and combine them with cocktail recipes from women bartenders around the world.

Legeron, Isabelle. *Natural Wine: An Introduction to Organic and Biodynamic Wines Made Naturally*. 2nd ed., New York: CICO Books, 2017.
This updated version of Legeron's 2014 volume remains the perfect primer on low-intervention, organic, and/or biodynamic wines and winemaking.

Martineau, Chantal. *How the Gringos Stole Tequila: The Modern Age of Mexico's Most Traditional Spirit.* Chicago, IL: Chicago Review Press, 2015.

Journalist Martineau pulls no punches as she travels through Mexico's agave heartlands, finding the best and worst products of a clash between capitalism, ancestral products, human rights, and a thirsty public.

Minnick, Fred. *Whiskey Women: The Untold Story of How Women Saved Bourbon, Scotch, and Irish Whiskey.* Lincoln, NE: Potomac Books, 2013.

The seminal text on the long and illustrious history of women in the whisk(e)y trade, from ancient Sumer to the present. I could never have said it better myself.

Newman, Kara. *Road Soda: Recipes and Techniques for Making Great Cocktails, Anywhere.* Brooklyn, NY: Dovetail, 2017.

———. *Shake. Stir. Sip. More Than 50 Effortless Cocktails Made in Equal Parts.* San Francisco, CA: Chronicle Books, 2016.

Drinks writer Newman collects simple recipes for the home cocktail enthusiast, to make portable cocktails and equal parts ones, respectively.

Perozzi, Chirstina, and Hallie Beaune. *The Naked Pint: An Unadulterated Guide to Craft Beer.* New York: Perigee, 2012.

Authors of the *Beer Chicks* blog give a down-to-earth primer on craft beer.

Petraske, Sasha, and Georgette Moger-Petraske. *Regarding Cocktails.* London: Phaidon Press, 2016.

After the tragic early death of cocktail pioneer Sasha Petraske, his widow, writer Georgette Moger-Petraske, undertook to complete the cocktail book he had planned but did not have the chance to write. Drawing on dozens of luminaries of the drinks world, Moger-Petraske's text shines as a labor of love for the man and the culture he embodied.

Reiner, Julie, and Kaitlyn Goalen. *The Craft Cocktail Party: Delicious Drinks for Every Occasion.* New York: Grand Central Life & Style, 2015.

Cocktail scene matriarch Reiner lays out in this beautiful volume how to create craft cocktails for just about any occasion.

Robinson, Jancis. *The Oxford Companion to Wine*. 4th ed., Oxford: Oxford University Press, 2015.

——. *The 24-Hour Wine Expert*. New York: Abrams Image, 2016.
Possibly the world's most respected wine critic, Robinson's canon is vast, but these two selections bookend the spectrum of desired wine knowledge for the complete novice to the professional.

Ross, Marissa A. *Wine. All the Time. The Casual Guide to Confident Drinking*. New York: Plume, 2017.
Ross's straightforward take to wine without the pretension is a favorite of bartenders and hobbyists alike.

Schaap, Rosie. *Drinking with Men: A Memoir*. New York: Riverhead Books, 2013.
Longtime New York drinks columnist Schaap details a life spent in and behind bars in this hilarious memoir.

Stewart, Amy. *The Drunken Botanist: The Plants That Create the World's Great Drinks*. Chapel Hill, NC: Algonquin Books, 2013.
Stewart's entrancing passion for her subjects makes this catalog of all the plants used in alcohol production—their history, medicinal properties, and boozy uses—a fast read that your friends will tire of you telling them about. Until, that is, they read it themselves.

Valenzuela-Zapata, Ana G., and Gary Paul Nabhan. *Tequila: A Natural and Cultural History*. Tucson: University of Arizona Press, 2004.
Agronomist and tequila industry insider Valenzuela-Zapata and ethnobotanist Nabhan take a plant's-eye view into the history of and controversies around Mexican distilling traditions.

Acknowledgments

Everything herein is due to the hard work of Olivia Taylor Smith and the team at Unnamed Press, who will have my gratitude forever. Great thanks to Sutipong Suruttanond, Melissa Ocampo, Fie Aljunied, Andrew and Katie Cooper, Andrea Caruso, Stuart Muller and Julie Padowski, Nader Beizaei, and Toni Goehring for being my GoFundMe angels and to Deborah and Peter Ewing who made everything possible from the start. I hope you all enjoy your signature cocktails. Also to Lou Amdur for the natural and unusual recommendations, spot-on as always. Big thanks to the taxpayers of Los Angeles for the Wi-Fi, office space, and research materials at the LAPL Los Feliz Branch Library, as well as the proprietors of Bolt EaHo. To Sam Distefano, the original Boss Lady, and Austin Mendez (nerd!), I'll always appreciate being indoctrinated into the industry by woke and caring bosses. Tuan Lee is the fuel and the fire and kept me alive during this process. Most important, thank you to the phenomenal individuals who gave their time and their stories to this volume: you're inspiring the next generation of booze nerds of all genders. As Joy Spence might say, big up to you.

Photo Credit: Tuan Lee

About Hope Ewing

Hope Ewing grew up in a haunted house surrounded by forest and sheep pastures in western New York State. After a decade raising money for New York City arts organizations, she received an MFA in creative writing from Columbia University and promptly moved to Los Angeles, where she finally became serious about bartending. Combining the twin passions of writing and drinking, she seeks to illuminate how intoxication and culture intersect, for better and for worse. Her work appears in *Punch*, *Serious Eats*, and other fine publications. She lives in LA with her partner and step-Chihuahua, and her favorite drink is all of them.

About Natalka Burian

Natalka Burian is the co-owner of two bars, Elsa and Ramona, as well as the co-founder of The Freya Project, a feminist fundraising reading series. She is the author of *Welcome to the Slipstream*, a novel, and *A Woman's Drink*, a cocktail book. She received an MA from Columbia University, and lives in Brooklyn with her husband and two daughters.

@unnamedpress

facebook.com/theunnamedpress

unnamedpress.tumblr.com

www.unnamedpress.com

@unnamedpress